STRONGER
than stress

BIBLE STUDY

DEVELOPING 10 SPIRITUAL PRACTICES TO WIN THE BATTLE OF OVERWHELM

BARB ROOSE

Revell

a division of Baker Publishing Group
Grand Rapids, Michigan

Published by Revell
a division of Baker Publishing Group
Grand Rapids, Michigan
RevellBooks.com

Printed in the United States of America

Library of Congress Cataloging-in-Publication Data
Names: Roose, Barbara L., author.
Title: Stronger than stress Bible study : developing 10 spiritual practices to win the battle of overwhelm / Barb Roose.
Description: Grand Rapids, Michigan : Revell, a division of Baker Publishing Group, [2024] | Includes bibliographical references.
Identifiers: LCCN 2023056463 | ISBN 9780800744922 (paper) | ISBN 9781493445615 (ebook)
Subjects: LCSH: Stress (Psychology)—Religious aspects—Christianity. | Stress management—Religious aspects—Christianity. | Spiritual life—Christianity.
Classification: LCC BV4509.5 .R663 2024 | DDC 248.8/6—dc23/eng/20240206
LC record available at https://lccn.loc.gov/2023056463

Unless otherwise indicated, Scripture quotations are from the *Holy Bible*, New Living Translation. Copyright © 1996, 2004, 2015 by Tyndale House Foundation. Used by permission of Tyndale House Publishers, Carol Stream, Illinois 60188. All rights reserved.

Scripture quotations labeled MSG are from *The Message*. Copyright © 1993, 2002, 2018 by Eugene H. Peterson. Used by permission of NavPress. All rights reserved. Represented by Tyndale House Publishers.

This publication is intended to provide helpful and informative material on the subjects addressed. Readers should consult their personal health professionals before adopting any of the suggestions in this book or drawing inferences from it. The author and publisher expressly disclaim responsibility for any adverse effects arising from the use or application of the information contained in this book.

Cover design by Mumtaz Mustafa Design

Published in association with Books & Such Literary Management, www.BooksAndSuch.com.

Baker Publishing Group publications use paper produced from sustainable forestry practices and postconsumer waste whenever possible.

24 25 26 27 28 29 30   7 6 5 4 3 2 1

STRONGER
than stress

BIBLE STUDY

Video Lesson Access

Link: https://barbroose.com/strongerthanstress/

CONTENTS

INTRODUCTION

Which one of the following phrases captures your thoughts as of late?

I can't do all of this.
If anything else happens, I'm going to have a stroke.
I want to cry.

None of us want to live this way. Living stressed-out is exhausting and discouraging. When we're overwhelmed, that overflows into complicating our relationships with others and lowers our capacity to take care of ourselves. This isn't the life that we want.

If this describes what you've experienced lately, I'm glad that you're here. I know this about you: you are doing the very best you can in a life where you have too much to do and too little time to do it. You're showing up with the best fight that you've got, but it's hard to hang in there with too many plates spinning, too little sleep, and probably too much coffee. None of us want to spend our lives trying to hold everything together but feeling like we're always about to fall apart. What would it mean for our lives to be different?

Today is the start of a new day. I don't know what prompted you to pick up this study, but I believe that it is God's invitation to you to exchange your stress for His all-surpassing peace.

A common dictionary description of overwhelm is a sensation of being buried or drowning, feeling defeated, and being unable to know what to do next. But here is my practical definition of overwhelm: *having too much to do with not enough time to do it, and feeling unsure, paralyzed, or stuck on how to fix it or move forward.*

In one study from the American Psychological Association, more than one-quarter of respondents reported feeling so stressed that they were unable to make decisions or keep up with their responsibilities. Other respondents reported that high stress contributed to their inability to concentrate, forgetfulness, and difficulty making decisions.[1]

Stress and overwhelm are a part of everyday life. Just because you love Jesus doesn't mean that you won't feel stress or battle it, nor should you condemn yourself or others for facing this struggle. Good news! God provides powerful, life-transforming tools so that you aren't helpless in this battle. In this six-week Bible study, you'll learn new, Scripture-based practices that will deepen your connection with God. As you learn new rhythms of growing in Christ, you'll trade the discouragement of overwhelm for the divine strength to live as an overcomer!

For decades, I believed that overwhelm was normal. It was normal for me to hear "I'm stressed" from the people around me. I never questioned whether there was another path apart from stress-eating, irritability, exhaustion, wanting to escape from my life, and regular burnout. At least once a year, I'd spend a few weeks or months sobbing and wishing that I could escape my life because I was tired of running myself into the ground and burning out. My life took a new direction when I signed up for a yearlong women's leadership discipleship group at my church. It was there that I first learned about spiritual practices. We called them *spiritual disciplines* back then. I didn't care what they were called, I knew that I needed to do something differently so that I could withstand the stress in my life. That experience was a game changer in my ability to open myself up to connecting with God better.

Instead of insisting that I had to set myself on fire in order to keep up with everything or try to be everything for everyone in my life, the spiritual practices taught me how to slow down, savor God's presence, and experience the safety and security of God's love and grace through the transforming power of the Holy Spirit.

In this Bible study, I want to create that same life-transforming experience for you. The invitation to experience more of God's peace awaits.

Our guide will be the apostle Paul. He was a first-century pastor, church planter, and prolific writer of many New Testament letters, and most notably, Paul considered himself a humble follower of Jesus Christ. Paul faced angry mobs, relational conflict, shipwrecks, physical threats, beatings, imprisonment, and court cases. What's wild is that those stressful circumstances came *after* he began following Jesus.

Paul is honest about life's challenging circumstances, but still, he intentionally calls us to have greater devotion and faith in Christ. We'll learn about how to do this from his example, his teachings, and his story. During the first week of the study, we'll learn about Paul's life and we'll look at how stress and overwhelm impact our lives, including our faith. Starting with the second week of the study, we'll begin to explore two new spiritual practices each week.

Week 1: Overview of Paul's Life and the Impact of Overwhelm

Week 2: Surrender and Sabbath

Week 3: Prayer and Scripture

Week 4: Simplicity and Self-Care

Week 5: Submission and Sacrifice

Week 6: Sisterhood and Celebration

That's an overview of our time together over the next six weeks. This is a journey that will require you to trust that God is at work. If you are willing, God will work in your heart, mind, and life. The beautiful truth about your healing is that it is already waiting for you because it has already been won. Jesus already accomplished this victory for you. It's waiting if you are willing. Winning the battle of overwhelm looks like living with a calm heart and a peaceful mind. As a result, you live from the power of God's peace so that you can participate in God's eternal purpose.

About the Study

This is a six-week Bible study with five lessons per week. The daily lessons will include a Scripture reading, questions, and daily guided prayer. In addition, there are practical suggestions and reflection questions along the way to guide you in implementing the new spiritual practices into your life.

The daily lessons will take fifteen to twenty minutes each. You'll need a Bible, a pen, and a willingness to listen and let God work in your heart and mind. You can do these lessons alone or in a group.

If you are meeting in a group, the lessons prepare you for a life-giving, spiritually rich discussion time together.

Video Teaching Sessions

There are six video teaching sessions included with this study. You'll watch each video after completing the corresponding weekly lessons. To access the videos, visit BarbRoose.com/StrongerThanStress or scan the QR code here or at the front of the book.

I've also prepared a complimentary listening guide that includes group discussion questions to accompany the video teaching lessons. You can download the listening guide in the same location as the teaching videos.

Creating a Safe Environment

In group settings, one of the difficulties in establishing connection is the fear of being judged, not having the right answers, or being ashamed. I believe that the small group environment is one of God's most precious gifts to us in our lives as believers. Not only do we experience the life-transforming power of the Scriptures as we read and study the Bible together, but as we share with each other, we can experience community, safety, and healing.

To create a safe environment that enables life transformation and healing, it's valuable to agree on some safety guidelines so that you and your group members can share what's really going on inside of you and in your lives. Here are a few values that you can share with your group. If you agree on these values, then I suggest that you read them at the start of each meeting for the first two weeks of the group. Then you can refer back to the list if needed as the study continues. These are not rules but guides so that everyone feels empowered and safe.

1. Everything that we say or hear stays in our group.
2. Say what you mean, mean what you say, but don't say it meanly.
3. Advice, opinions, or suggestions can be requested but not offered.
4. Keep coming back, even if your homework isn't complete.
5. Safe responses after someone shares include: "Thank you for sharing." "We're glad that you're here." "We believe that God will help you figure this out."
6. God knows all the details, so we don't need to overshare with the group.

A Final Word

I'm glad that we're starting out on this journey together! There's nothing like studying God's Word in community. I'm honored that you are joining me for this Bible study experience. I will be praying for you!

One final encouragement: God gives us a wealth of options, including counseling and medication, to equip us in dealing with mental health concerns such as stress, anxiety, and depression. If your level of stress or a related condition interferes with the quality of your life or relationships, you are encouraged to seek medical attention and intervention.

Too Many
Spinning Plates

MEMORY VERSE

Now may the Lord of peace himself give you his peace at all times and in every situation.

2 Thessalonians 3:16

GOD CARES ABOUT YOU

My kids never saw it coming. They'd spent the day asking for snacks and demanding that I referee disagreements over screen time. I could feel my temperature rising throughout the day. There was laundry heaped on the couch, dinner waiting to go into the oven, and my phone buzzing with text messages from work. My mind looked like a room of spinning plates as I calculated how I could finish dinner, clean up the house, figure out my work presentation, and find time to work out before climbing in bed by 10 p.m. *How can I do it all when there's too much to get done?*

"Mom . . . Mom . . . MOM!!!!"

That last "Mom" did it.

"Kids, get down here!"

My crew tumbled down into the kitchen. They jockeyed for the position farthest away from a mother who looked like she was about to blow. They weren't wrong. I was too frazzled to fix anything, but desperation inspired me to one thing. I informed them that my name was no longer Mom.

"For the rest of the day, you will call me . . . Betty."

Fifteen years later, my kids still laugh about "call me Betty" day. I now laugh about it too. But back then, the constant stress and overwhelm weren't funny.

My life looked like a giant room of spinning plates, and I felt like everything was all on me. I ran from one responsibility to the next. One problem to the next. Heart pounding, blood racing, I never felt like I could catch up or get ahead. On that one day in my kitchen, I couldn't quit my responsibilities, nor did I want to. Out of desperation, I could change my name from Mom to Betty.

Anytime we feel the sensation of being stretched too thin, drowning in our responsibilities, or being unable to know what to do next, all of that is overwhelm. My personal definition of overwhelm is *having too much to do with not enough time to do it, and feeling unsure, paralyzed, or stuck on how to fix it or move forward.*

Overwhelm can show up instantly, like a medical crisis or a spouse who dies unexpectedly. For most of us, however, overwhelm builds and then crushes us all at once. No matter how it happens, no one is happy in overwhelm. You're not enjoying your relationships, your faith, or your life when it all feels like too much and you don't know what to do about it.

This week, you'll discover that God meets you right in the middle of all the plates that you're spinning in your life. You'll be reminded through Scripture how much you are seen and loved even though life seems so chaotic right now. You'll also meet the apostle Paul, our guide for this journey. As someone who lived through constant stress and times of overwhelm, Paul offers us great wisdom and grace to begin the quest to win the battle of overwhelm.

What times during the day do you feel a wave of overwhelm or stress creeping in? What is hard for you about dealing with overwhelm?

Think about the analogy of spinning plates. In the space below, list some of the plates that you have spinning in your life (e.g., to-dos, unsolved problems, crisis, unmet dreams, prayer requests). Draw an arrow beside the ones that feel especially overwhelming to you right now and write why that is.

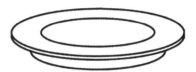

God sees each one of those plates, and more than that, He sees your heart and your overwhelm. Rest assured, God is concerned about you and He sees you right now. We'll catch up with Paul in tomorrow's lesson, but I want to share a prayer from King David that feels appropriate for the starting point in your journey. David wrote this prayer after his own son tried to overthrow his kingdom. Underline any words or phrases that resonate with you.

> Listen to my prayer, O God.
>> Do not ignore my cry for help!
> Please listen and answer me,
>> for I am overwhelmed by my troubles. . . .
>
> My heart pounds in my chest.
>> The terror of death assaults me.
> Fear and trembling overwhelm me,
>> and I can't stop shaking. (Ps. 55:1–2, 4–5)

Even King David, who was called a man after God's own heart, experienced seasons in life when it was all too much. Rather than turning away from God in the middle of his problems, David turned toward God. Notice David's real and raw emotions. He doesn't hide them from God, and you don't have to either. David doesn't complain, but he does express how he feels. God welcomes you to do the same.

King David continues to pour out his heart but ends by proclaiming this truth:

> Give your burdens to the LORD,
>   and he will take care of you.
>   He will not permit the godly to slip and fall. (Ps. 55:22)

What encouragement do you draw from David's words for wherever you are today?

MEMORY VERSE MOMENT

Each day, you'll engage with the memory verse in different ways to help you embed these powerful words in your heart and mind.

Write this week's memory verse in the space below. Circle the words that stand out to you and make note of situations that apply next to what you circled.

PRAYER

God, thank You for inviting me to be honest with You about the places in my life where I feel overwhelmed and scared. As I begin this journey, I choose to proclaim King David's words and believe that You will take care of me and show me the path to Your grace. In Jesus's name, amen.

PAUL GETS IT

Five different times the Jewish leaders gave me thirty-nine lashes. Three times I was beaten with rods. Once I was stoned. Three times I was shipwrecked. Once I spent a whole night and a day adrift at sea. I have traveled on many long journeys. I have faced danger from rivers and from robbers. I have faced danger from my own people, the Jews, as well as from the Gentiles. I have faced danger in the cities, in the deserts, and on the seas. And I have faced danger from men who claim to be believers but are not. I have worked hard and long, enduring many sleepless nights. I have been hungry and thirsty and have often gone without food. I have shivered in the cold, without enough clothing to keep me warm.

2 Corinthians 11:24–27

We like to be sure a person knows what they are talking about before we're willing to listen to them. When it comes to stress and overwhelm, perhaps you want to be sure someone knows how you feel before you're willing to listen to them.

Read 2 Corinthians 11:24–27 at the beginning of today's lesson. List three or four stressful situations that Paul faced as a missionary for Jesus.

Imagine yourself as Paul in one of those situations. What might have been stressful or overwhelming for you?

It's hard to imagine one person encountering all of Paul's difficulties. In our first-world modern culture, these are not the same types of stressful circumstances that we normally encounter in our faith today. However, there are believers around the world who face persecution and hardship at this very moment.

The next part of Paul's message to the believers in Corinth might come as a surprise, but I hope it helps you recognize that Paul's words relate to your life too.

Read 2 Corinthians 11:28–29. What emotions does Paul express?

In a move that would have shocked his highly educated audience, Paul admits to experiencing anxiety and anger. He's anxious about how his church plants are doing. He's also angry about the attacks that the believers are facing. Admitting to such strong emotions would have been contrary to the popular teachings of the Stoics, who had a great deal of influence at the time. The Stoics believed that success was learning how to face stress, anxiety, or fear without expressing emotion.[1]

Where have you encountered stress or overwhelm because of your faith?

There are times when living for Jesus means that your choices and actions will conflict with the world. While it's tempting to act powerful and boastful like Paul's enemies in Corinth, Paul shares an upside-down approach with the believers. This approach offers a key first step toward winning your battle with overwhelm.

Read 2 Corinthians 11:30. What does Paul say that he will boast about instead?

Rather than thrusting out his chest and insisting that nothing bothers him or preening like a peacock and pretending he knows it all, Paul owns the fact that he doesn't have to have all the answers, nor does he need to pretend that life isn't hard. Paul believes his authenticity is what allows God's miraculous glory to shine through his life.

There are two key takeaways as you gear up for God to help you win the battle of overwhelm.

First, you don't need to have all the answers for everything. Stop putting that pressure on yourself. God knows everything that you don't know. Best of all, you can trust Him.

Second, you can take off the mask, the cape, or anything else that keeps you from showing up as your real self. You don't need to pretend or stuff your emotions. God loves the real you.

Paul's upside-down strategy means that the more honest you are about your overwhelm and the more you're willing to let God help you, the more victory you will experience in the battle of overwhelm or any other battle in your life.

As you complete today's lesson and reflect on today's takeaways, write down anything that has encouraged you.

MEMORY VERSE MOMENT

Practice today by filling in the blanks:

Now may the Lord of _____ himself give you his peace at
_____ _____ and in _____ situation.

2 Thessalonians 3:16

PRAYER

God, thank You for guiding me toward this study experience. As I learn about Paul's background, I am reminded that You never waste any detail or situation in our lives. I'm open today for You to suggest something from my past that reminds me of Your presence or Your love for me. In Jesus's name, amen.

PAUL'S BEGINNINGS

Then Paul said, "I am a Jew, born in Tarsus, a city in Cilicia, and I was brought up and educated here in Jerusalem under Gamaliel. As his student, I was carefully trained in our Jewish laws and customs. I became very zealous to honor God in everything I did, just like all of you today."

Acts 22:3

Today, we're rewinding back to the beginning of Paul's life. Now that you've studied some of the difficulties that he went through, you might be curious about the early parts of Paul's life that started his journey to Jesus.

Since Paul's name isn't mentioned in the New Testament until after Jesus's ascension, it's easy to assume that he wasn't born until after Jesus's time on earth. But Paul was born around AD 6 and was given the Jewish name Saul (Acts 7:58; 13:9), making him a contemporary of Jesus. As far as what's revealed in Scripture, there are no recorded mentions of any interactions between Jesus and Paul in Jerusalem or the surrounding country. Paul's meeting with Jesus would come later, about two years after Jesus's ascension to heaven. For now, let's learn a little more about Paul's early life and discover more about the man who would endure so many hardships.

Read Acts 22:3 and Philippians 3:5–6. Fill in the blanks on the next page with details from Paul's life.

Paul was a member of the tribe of _____. (Phil. 3:5)

He was born in _____. (Acts 22:3)

Paul was educated in _____ under _____.
(Acts 22:3)

He was a member of the strict _____. (Phil. 3:5)

In Acts 22:3 and Philippians 3:6, how does Paul describe his dedication to his religion?

According to scholars, Paul was born into a middle-class Jewish family in the city of Tarsus in what is modern-day Turkey. Tarsus was an important city of the ancient world, ranking right up there with Athens and Alexandria. As an interesting detail of ancient pop culture, Tarsus was also the place where Antony and Cleopatra first met in 41 BC.[2]

While it's true that God would sometimes change people's names in the Bible—for example, Abram to Abraham, Sarai to Sarah, and Jacob to Israel—God did not change Saul's name to Paul. Rather, Saul is the Hebrew name he was given at birth, and Paul was his Greek name. After his encounter with Jesus on the road to Damascus, Paul began using his Greek name. This is symbolic of his divine assignment to preach the gospel to Gentiles and not just to Jews.

In two of his New Testament letters, Paul details his Jewish lineage and explains that he is from the tribe of Benjamin, the same tribe as King Saul, the most notable person from that tribe in the Old Testament (Rom. 11:1; Phil. 3:5). While we don't know if his parents had Israel's first king in mind when they named their son, Paul was proud of his Jewish heritage.

Paul's education under Gamaliel was extensive and sharpened his understanding of the Scriptures. That knowledge would become an important foundation for Paul in later years as he shared the gospel with Jewish people who didn't know Jesus. Paul could explain how Jesus fulfilled the law in a way that they could understand.

In addition to his Jewish heritage, Paul had another important distinction that he would leverage at key times during difficult circumstances in his life.

Read Acts 22:27–28. What is Paul's other association?

As you read Acts 22:28, notice how the commander had to purchase his Roman citizenship, but Paul declares that he was born a Roman citizen. Being a Roman citizen from birth meant Paul enjoyed an elevated status. This would come in handy as Paul faced one difficulty after another. Paul's Roman citizenship also opened doors for God to use him in unique, even miraculous circumstances, like being sent to Rome, the center of the first-century world, to speak to Caesar.

In Paul's time, Roman citizenships weren't automatically handed out. Some sources indicate that a person had to be born in a certain area of the empire to receive citizenship, whereas other sources suggest that someone in Paul's family may have performed some type of service that the empire deemed valuable and the family received Roman citizenship as a reward.[3]

Already, we can see how the background of Paul's early life makes a fascinating foundation for his future ministry.

In tomorrow's lesson, we'll learn about Paul's journey from being a Pharisee to a Jesus-follower, and we'll look at some principles of grace that we need to remember when we're overwhelmed.

What did you learn today about Paul's life that was interesting or intriguing to you?

MEMORY VERSE MOMENT

Practice today by filling in the blanks:

Now may the _____ _____ _____ himself give you _____ _____ at all times and in _____ _____.

2 Thessalonians 3:16

PRAYER

God, as I reflect on this week's memory verse, remind me that when I focus on You, I will experience Your perfect peace. Today, I'm stressed about _____. Help me to keep my focus on You rather than my circumstances, to-do list, anxiety, or fears. I choose to trust that You will provide the grace and peace that I need for today. In Jesus's name, amen.

OVERWHELMED BY GOD

I have told you all this so that you may have peace in me. Here on earth you will have many trials and sorrows. But take heart, because I have overcome the world.

John 16:33

I spent a lifetime as a Christian always striving to do more because I thought that's what God wanted from me. Read my Bible more. Pray more. Serve more. Give more. I tried my best. If you know what I'm talking about, chances are you know how exhausting it can be to spin plates because you think that's what God wants you to do.

As a Pharisee, Paul embraced all the plate-spinning requirements of the law. As a Pharisee, Paul was passionate about making sure that all Jews followed the rules. After Jesus ascended to heaven, His followers began growing in number. The religious leaders in Jerusalem tasked Paul (referred to as Saul in today's reading) with traveling to Damascus to capture, imprison, and even kill Jewish people who had decided to follow Jesus.

Read Acts 9:1–6. What was Saul intending to do? (vv. 1–2)

What stops his travels? (v. 3)

What does Jesus mean when He says that Saul is persecuting Him? (v. 4)

As Saul travels to Damascus with his entourage, it's not hard to imagine him plotting how to find and arrest believers. He pats his bag with the letters from Jerusalem that give him authority to hound, punish, and even kill, if needed.

Then he sees the light—quite literally.

Saul is faced with a blinding light from heaven, but there is no way for him to block it. The light's power arrests his movement, and he falls to his knees. If that isn't jarring enough, Saul hears a loud voice speaking. Lying there on the ground, the man armed with the authority of the Jerusalem leaders is overwhelmed in the moment and asks a question that will change his life: "Who are you?"

Jesus brings immediate clarity to Saul's confusion. "I am Jesus, the one you are persecuting!" (v. 5).

While on the ground, Saul has a personal encounter with the power and authority of Jesus. Saul is overwhelmed by Jesus because God has greater plans for Saul's life. Saul's aim had been to snatch up the Jewish believers who accepted the gospel message, but Jesus tells Saul that He now oversees Saul's life. The authority in Saul's life has shifted from the Jerusalem leaders to Jesus.

Read Acts 9:7–19. What is Saul's condition after Jesus speaks to him?

It's not unreasonable to think that Saul would be in shock after his encounter with Jesus. What do you suppose he might have been thinking about or feeling during that time? (There's no wrong answer, just your opinion.)

What is Ananias's concern? (vv. 13–14)

What does God tell Ananias about Saul? (vv. 15–16)

After Saul is led to Damascus by his traveling companions, God speaks to a man named Ananias and tells him about Saul. After his initial fearful hesitation, Ananias goes to Saul, lays hands on him, and relays the message from God. Saul regains his sight and is baptized.

The first word that God says to Ananias is "go." He doesn't address Ananias's questions; His instruction "go" is enough to communicate that if God is sending him, then Ananias will have a God who will go with him, no matter what happens.

Do you ever wish that God would just tell you how things will turn out? We like to think that knowing all the details will eliminate our stress. If we knew the details, we could plan better or we could protect ourselves or the ones we love. If we knew the details, we could track our progress and even do our part to make sure we get to the happy payout. However, God knows that faith is more valuable to our life journey than facts. Knowing information is good, but learning to keep our eyes on God is better, especially because the facts may lead to hardships or difficulties.

What are some of the things God has called you to do but you feel stressed about doing? (Examples: forgiveness, a big faith step, tithing, a difficult conversation)

Stress is the body's internal response to external pressure. Whenever something in our environment shifts, our bodies pick up on it before we register it in our minds. These triggers, what I call "stress starters," aren't guaranteed to cause stress, but they do contribute to the roots of stress. There are four stress starters:

- Uncertain—feeling unstable or insecure about an outcome or future

- Unexpected—being taken by surprise and unable to process or adjust

- Uncontrollable—being unable to manage or fix the situation

- Uncomfortable—feeling uneasy and bothered by what's happening

Which of these is a source of stress in your life right now? Remember, these don't have to be bad sources of stress. Sometimes good things can cause stress too. Where would you place the sources in the stress starters list below?

Four Stress Starters	Situation, person, or circumstance
Uncertain	
Unexpected	
Uncontrollable	
Uncomfortable	

What are the common symptoms of stress that you're dealing with? Rate on a scale of 1 (none) to 5 (extreme).

Difficulty sleeping	1	2	3	4	5
Irritability	1	2	3	4	5
Frequent crying	1	2	3	4	5
Hard time concentrating	1	2	3	4	5
Overeating	1	2	3	4	5
Undereating	1	2	3	4	5
Disconnection from God	1	2	3	4	5
Withdrawing from others	1	2	3	4	5

Read John 16:33 at the start of today's lesson. Circle the word "overcome" and underline "trials and sorrows." In the first sentence, before Jesus even mentions our trials and sorrows, what does He say He wants us to have?

P_____ in m_____.

In the Old Testament, the Hebrew word for peace is *shalom*.[4] We usually associate peace with calm and quiet, but *shalom* is so much more. It means wholeness. The New Testament Greek equivalent of shalom is *eiréné*.[5] One source expands the definition of *eiréné* to mean "having it all together" and an "inner rest." Peace isn't the absence of trouble; in fact, the existence of peace recognizes that trouble is around. There's a famous piece of art that depicts a bird settled and sleeping in a nest tucked into the side of a cliff as a torrential rainstorm rages all around. That's peace.

As you reflect on the definition of peace, either *shalom* or *eiréné*, put those definitions in your own words.

Describe a stressful time or season in your life when you experienced Jesus's peace.

God doesn't minimize your hardships. But God's goal is to keep guiding us toward Him, which keeps us from finding ourselves stuck in the stressful circumstances of daily life.

As you consider Jesus's promise of peace, what hope does that give you for whatever you're facing today?

MEMORY VERSE MOMENT

Today, you will fill in the back half of your memory verse:

Now may the Lord of peace himself give you his peace _____ _____

_____ _____ ____ _____ _____.

2 Thessalonians 3:16

PRAYER

God, as my mind is spinning on my complicated life, remind me that You've already spoken Your peace over every worry, care, and concern. In Jesus's name, amen.

GRACE IS ENOUGH

So to keep me from becoming proud, I was given a thorn in my flesh, a messenger from Satan to torment me and keep me from becoming proud. Three different times I begged the Lord to take it away.

2 Corinthians 12:7–8

Read 2 Corinthians 12:7–8 above. What did Satan give Paul to torment him?

What was the purpose of the affliction?

How many times did Paul pray for God to take it away?

Maybe you're picturing a thorn on a rose bush, but the Greek word Paul uses could also be translated as "tent stake."[6] Ouch. Some scholars speculate that Paul's thorn might have been an eye ailment or skin affliction, while others suggest it was harassment from opponents or a struggle with sinful thoughts. Since Paul doesn't give details, all we can know is that his affliction tormented him. He prayed numerous times for healing. One commenter suggests that when Paul writes that he prayed three times, it may have been a figure of speech for praying continuously.[7]

What happened that God wanted to keep Paul from becoming proud? Fourteen years prior to writing to the Corinthians, Paul saw visions and revelations from God that he describes as "so astounding that they cannot be expressed in words" (2 Cor. 12:4). He didn't write about this vision from God until over a decade after it happened. If I'd had such an experience, I'd be all over social media saying, "Guess what I dreamed about last night!" The only reason Paul wrote to the believers was because of the arrogant gospel preachers in their midst. After his personal encounter with Jesus and those astounding dreams, Paul could have become one of them.

Satan may have inflicted the thorn in Paul's flesh, but the root cause was God's decision to allow Paul to experience something difficult to keep him from experiencing something more damaging: pride. What Satan meant for evil, God used for Paul's good. God didn't want Paul's mountaintop experience to plant seeds of self-applause or self-sufficiency.

What is your "thorn in the flesh" that you've prayed for God to remove but He hasn't?

Has living in that difficult or sometimes overwhelming situation drawn you closer to God or pushed you away? In what ways?

For years, I begged God each day to remove an addiction that had taken hold of someone in our home. It was a thorn stuck into the flesh closest to my heart. With every breath I took, that thorn hurt, but I couldn't move it. Perhaps you're in a season of life right now where you know exactly how that feels.

I didn't think I could survive unless that overwhelming problem went away. But year after year, I had to face it each day. In time, God brought people into my life to help me. Most of all, I learned such an important lesson about the sustaining power of God's grace.

Read 2 Corinthians 12:9–10 and write out verse 9 below. Circle what God told Paul was enough.

Why does Paul boast about his weakness? (v. 10)

Grace. This is what God gives us in stressful circumstances or times of suffering when life and even God's ways don't make sense. God's grace is "God's provision for our every need when we need it."[8]

Grace paves the way for God's peace. Notice how God doesn't say that we are to provide for our every need. He tells us that He will provide, and our part is to receive. God's grace can look like special friends who encourage us to keep trusting Him, surprise blessings, or occasions of celebration to lift our hearts in between the long days of dealing with our situation.

One of the women in my pilot group for this study shared the following observation: "If Paul didn't have miraculous healing and he learned to live by grace, then I can too. The big question for me is this: Is God's glory worth all the pain that I go through? I know that God doesn't inflict pain to get glory. He can use my pain, redeem it, and make something beautiful come from it."

From what we know about Paul, that affliction would have added a layer of difficulty to the already stressful circumstances he was experiencing, yet Paul never writes about that affliction ever again. That doesn't mean Paul wasn't facing trouble or stress. Paul learned to live in the abundance of God's grace rather than give the power to his ongoing problem.

What's the key to experiencing God's grace? Receiving it. Letting God's grace flow into your life instead of staying closed off because God hasn't fixed your problem.

MEMORY VERSE MOMENT

Here's your chance! As you wrap up this week's study, you've had the opportunity to review the memory verse multiple times. Now, complete the memory verse by writing it out in the space below.

PRAYER

God, thank You for the gift of grace, especially in the circumstances that haven't changed. God, help me to live through it one day at a time. When the pain or stress feels too great, please remind me that Your grace is enough and help me to open my heart and hands to say yes to receiving it. In Jesus's name, amen.

Getting Out
of Survival Mode

MEMORY VERSE

Keep putting into practice all you learned and received from me—
everything you heard from me and saw me doing. Then the God
of peace will be with you.

Philippians 4:9

INTRODUCTION TO SPIRITUAL PRACTICES

In a world that can be overwhelming on the outside, Paul guides us toward the path where we can invite God's Holy Spirit to strengthen us on the inside. Rather than telling us to follow religious rules that cannot address our inner anxiety, control issues, and the pressure of time or stress, Paul teaches believers about how to let the Holy Spirit transform our lives by being willing to let God's way of life reshape us. As the Holy Spirit changes the way we think, the stress reactions that push against our insides will instead be transformed to strength and peace.

With a pastoral heart and a passion for the gospel, Paul wrote to believers in churches all over the ancient world. He may not have used the term "spiritual practices," but his writings tell us what following Jesus should look like. Like the words "Trinity" and "discipleship," the terms "spiritual practices" and "spiritual disciplines" aren't in the Bible, but the principles behind the practices are everywhere in Paul's writings. Today we'll learn why spiritual practices are essential and see how Scripture supports the idea.

At first, you might wonder if these spiritual practices add more plates to your already busy life. However, you'll discover that when you create space for God, He reduces your overwhelm. Therefore, you aren't adding more activity to your life, you're making room for God to reduce your stress and overwhelm.

1. Spiritual practices focus on "how to be" training versus "how to do" training.

You are a human be-ing, not a human do-ing. This innermost part of you is what determines what you like or don't like, your passions and struggles. Your spirit is the unseen operating system that makes you who you are. While that identity informs what you will do, the starting point is recognizing that there is a "becoming journey" that you're on for your entire life. Your spirit is influenced by many factors, such as your family of origin either cheering for you or criticizing you, the good and bad things that happen to you, and your faith formation.

How your spirit is nurtured or neglected will be revealed in how you live your life.

Unfortunately, our inner selves don't receive much intentional training. Our focus is more often on outer, behavioral training, or what I call "how to do" training. Starting at birth, our outer selves receive the most training. It starts with sleep training, then potty training. Little kids receive training wheels for their bikes, and then there is driver's training for teenagers. Adults go through job training.

You know that there are parts of you that God wants to work out for His glory and your good. Only God can see all of you, and only He can see the entire big picture around you.

Read Psalm 139:13–14. What does the writer say about our humanity?

Psalm 139 reminds us how complex we are and how God knows us so well. Our spirits were created by God, who is Spirit. When we're willing to engage in spiritual practices, we create space for the God who knows us so well to bring to light what we can't see so that we can allow the Holy Spirit to rewire our thinking and emotions.

Read Psalm 139:23–24. What is the writer's prayer?

In Psalm 51:10, the writer's prayer identifies his deep desire for what type of heart?

Spiritual practices are a workout for your spirit—and sometimes they will make you sweat just like at the gym. Spiritual practices focus on training our inner selves. We can't train our inner selves, only God can. Either we're blind to our spiritual deficiencies or we're unwilling or unable to change them. Praise God that He can! The key is our willingness.

2. We don't perform spiritual practices *for* God, we participate in them *with* God.

God wants more *for* you than *from* you.

Just as you don't need to do anything to earn God's grace or salvation, you don't need to perform spiritual disciplines to earn God's favor, forgiveness, or anything else. You are God's precious masterpiece. He sent Jesus to die for you so that the price of sin could be paid and you could be made righteous, which opens the door to relationship with God.

One of the tensions we face in any discussion of spiritual practices is our tendency to place the emphasis on the outcome or the pursuit of perfection.

Read Romans 12:1–2. What does God want from us? What will He do for us?

Tomorrow we'll look at the first spiritual practice: surrender. This is the spiritual practice on which the other practices are built.

There are a lot of reasons we hold ourselves back from God. Sometimes it's out of pride in wanting to do life our own way. For many of us, we're like Adam and Eve in the garden after they ate from the tree. We're afraid or ashamed of our mistakes, our failures, our inability to get that one part of our life or that one sin under control. We're overwhelmed by our inability to be better Christians. What if God already knows this and is saying to you today, "Give Me all of you so that I can do what you can't do"?

You are a spirit created by a Spirit. For all your fear and running from God, He knows that you find peace when your spirit is connected to His.

Read James 4:8. What does God do in response to our intentional effort to connect with Him?

What did you learn today about the role of spiritual practices that is helpful for you to know?

MEMORY VERSE MOMENT

Write this week's memory verse in the space below. Circle the words that stand out to you and in the margin write any situations that apply to what you circled.

PRAYER

God, thank You for the means to nurture my spirit. Rather than creating us and leaving us to our own devices, You've made a way for us to intentionally and creatively connect with You. Continue to open my heart and pour in Your wisdom so that I can use these practices to know You more. In Jesus's name, amen.

GOD, I CAN'T BUT YOU CAN, SO I WILL LET YOU

SURRENDER

My Father! If it is possible, let this cup of suffering be taken away from me. Yet I want your will to be done, not mine.

Matthew 26:39

The spiritual practice of surrender is the foundation on which the other spiritual practices are built. This is a practice in which you give God permission to work in your life in the way that He needs to in order for you to experience the fullness of freedom in Christ. Before we go any further, let's establish the proper definition of surrender.

First, surrender is not giving up on someone or something. Letting go of control and letting God in doesn't mean that you stop caring or abandon what's important to you. Second, surrender is not giving in and agreeing to someone else's agenda, especially if they are manipulative or self-centered. Surrender does not ignore boundaries; in fact, it's often the practice of surrender that allows us to keep healthy boundaries.

Surrender is giving over to God what is out of your control and allowing Him to determine what's best. Giving over is recognizing that there's something you love, value, or want to protect and that you can't do it, but you know that God can.

The most classic picture of surrender is Jesus in the garden of Gethsemane as He prayed before being arrested, tried, and crucified.

Read Matthew 26:39–44. In the space below, write out the prayer that Jesus prayed. How many times did He pray it?

Why do you think that Jesus needed to pray that same prayer three times?

The spiritual practice of surrender gives you the opportunity to pray like Jesus, "I want your will to be done, not mine." Many things hinder us from practicing surrender, but the leader of the pack is often fear. We're afraid of what could happen or not happen if we let go of control. Our expectations can also hinder us. We may have a fixed view of how we want circumstances to flow or the way we think things should turn out. Other hindrances might be pride or a lack of trust in God. Regardless of what hinders us, when we hold on to everything, we eventually discover that we're in control of nothing, and we often find ourselves hit with a lot of overwhelm.

If letting go of control is hard for you, what are some of the reasons for that? What situations beyond your control are stressing you out?

The tension with surrender is that, while we do want God to work, we're afraid of what He might want to change or that He won't choose what we would choose. When we're faced with a stressful situation involving something or someone we love, are trying to protect, or are working hard to fix, our perspective narrows down into what we desire or feel is best. Then we push for that outcome. Surrender is hard because we don't know what God may do, but the following verse can bring you comfort.

Read Jeremiah 29:11 and write it in the space below.

This popular verse casts a vision for what I like to call God's Big Picture, which is His eternal perspective on our lives compared to our fixation on a single moment or season of our lives. Often, we hold on hard because we lose sight of a God who can make anything possible (Matt. 19:26), who watches over every detail of our lives (Matt. 6:26), and who is always at work for us (Phil. 1:6).

Surrender is hard when we forget who God is or shrink Him down to our human size.

Contrast this with our human point of view, which I call the small-screen perspective, like a cell phone. The problem with our cell phones is that they give us the illusion that we have power. We spend so much time looking down at our phones, but we've convinced ourselves that we can see the whole world. Just as cell phones only offer a small-screen view of knowledge or experience, we have only a limited view of ourselves and the world. Our limited life space also short-circuits our perspective compared to God's.

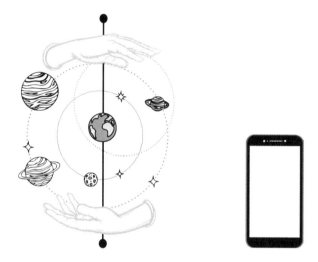

One of the most important shifts we can make in our human lives, especially as followers of Jesus, is to move from our small-screen perspective to God's Big Picture. This means that we see ourselves, our lives, and our circumstances through the lens of God's vast and mighty power, and we focus on His eternal perspective rather than what's happening to us in the moment.

Paul captures God's eternal perspective on our problems in his letter to the Romans. At this point in Paul's life, he has been through significant stressful events, so he's speaking from experience.

Read Romans 5:3–5. Write out the progression that Paul lays out for us:

Problems and trials → _____ → _____ →

_____

According to verse 5, what is God's attitude toward us?

In every moment and every situation of our lives, God is working in us, around us, and for us, but His Big Picture is eternity, which is a purpose beyond our problems in that moment. This means that God is using whatever we face for His purposes and His glory. That doesn't mean He ignores what we're going through. As you learned last week, God's grace is also more than enough when your circumstances aren't changing or your life goes in a different direction. Surrender is the only path to God's peace in those times.[1]

Jesus's prayer, "I want your will to be done, not mine," is the attitude of surrender. Jesus opened His hands and, despite intense stress and strain, gave over control to God of what would happen. We're reminded in Hebrews 12:2 that Jesus surrendered to God because He knew God's Big Picture for humanity and the salvation that we needed.

Surrender is a tough topic, especially when you sense God calling you to let go of something or someone important to you. Yet, if it's not in your control, the wisest and best move is to let go of stressing about it and to let go of meddling, and yield yourself, your circumstances, and the outcome over to God's control.

Tomorrow, you'll learn specific tools to help you practice surrender and create space for you to receive God's peace in exchange for what you can't control.

List the places in your life where you feel overwhelmed. Look at the list and put a checkmark by what you can control and an X by what you can't control.

☐ _____

☐ _____

☐ _____

☐ _____

☐ _____

MEMORY VERSE MOMENT

Fill in the blanks for this week's memory verse:

Keep _____ into _____ all you learned and received from me—everything you heard from me and saw me doing. Then the _____ ___ _____ will be with you.

Philippians 4:9

PRAYER

God, You can handle everything in my life that I cannot. Remind me to surrender what I can't control and to keep surrendering it when I forget and want to try to carry it all on my own. I give over my problems to You in exchange for Your peace. In Jesus's name, amen.

CREATING A SPIRITUAL PRACTICE OF SURRENDER

I pray that from his glorious, unlimited resources he will empower you with inner strength through his Spirit. Then Christ will make his home in your hearts as you trust in him. Your roots will grow down into God's love and keep you strong.

Ephesians 3:16–17

Read Ephesians 3:16–17. What are the benefits of giving God space to work in your life?

What do your roots grow deep into? What will that do for you?

Yesterday, you learned about surrender as giving over to God what is out of your control and allowing Him to determine what's best.

The practice of surrender equips you to give over and place into God's hands whatever you love, want to fix, or want to change—and leave it there. Once it's out of your hands, then God fills your hands with His peace. His peace allows you to live out His eternal purpose for you while He's working through your situation. God's peace protects you from getting worn down and worn out by worry, not taking care of yourself, and feeling hopeless if the outcome isn't as you'd hoped.

Today's lesson is interactive, so you'll use your study time to engage in the practices and reflect on them at the end of the lesson.

Practical Application #1: Begin with Prayer

First, envision whatever or whoever it is that you sense God calling you to surrender. There may be some emotions as you accept that you need to let it go. That's okay. It might be helpful for you to read today's closing prayer. Surrender is a healthy decision, and your fearful emotions might need time to adjust to a healthy decision. Don't let that deter you.

In this moment, what is God prompting you to surrender?

Next, pray this simple prayer: *God, I can't but You can, so I will let You. Amen.*

You can add more to this prayer if you'd like. Surrender may be easy for you, but chances are it will be highly emotionally charged, especially if you're afraid of letting go. Which brings up an important note: You may have all sorts of emotions while surrendering, even big emotions. That's okay. Remember, Jesus was sweating drops of blood in the garden of Gethsemane. What matters is following through with surrender no matter how you feel.

Practical Application #2: Palms Down, Palms Up Exercise

One spiritual exercise that offers you a way to act out the practice of surrender is "palms down, palms up."[2] Using those simple instructions, I've scripted the prayers for you.

1. Begin with your palms down as a gesture of release as you begin a surrender prayer. If you need words, you can use these:

   God, I give _____ to You because it is weighing down my mind or causing overwhelm. I release my fear of _____. I release using control-loving behaviors like _____ to force a solution or direct the outcome.

2. Take a few deep breaths and then turn your palms up to receive as you pray:

   God, I would like to receive Your promises. I recognize Your presence with me right now. I would like to receive Your peace about _____. I would like to receive Your patience with/ for _____. Like Jesus I pray, "I want your will to be done, not mine," God, and I trust You with the outcome. Amen.

Just as Jesus repeated His prayer multiple times in the garden, you may need to surrender repeatedly as the temptation to take control creeps in. However many times you need to pray that surrender prayer, what matters is that you keep praying it and giving it over to God.

This practice offers more than a tool to alleviate your overwhelm. When you place yourself, your circumstances, your loved ones, and your to-dos in God's hands, you'll experience God's hands working in every area of your life.

REFLECTION QUESTIONS

1. What are your takeaways from engaging in the practice of surrender?

2. Did you sense a connection or response from God? What was it?

3. Are there any adjustments that you could make so that this practice would be more meaningful and sustainable for you?

MEMORY VERSE MOMENT

Fill in the blanks for this week's memory verse:

Keep putting into practice _____ _____ _____ _____
_____ from me—everything you heard from me and saw me doing. Then the peace of God will be with you.

Philippians 4:9

PRAYER

God, it's hard to let go of what I can't control, but I choose to trust You. Work in my heart so that I am willing to surrender my life, my overwhelm, and any other specific matter to You. If You could create the universe, You can take care of everything else in my life. In Jesus's name, amen.

LETTING GOD WORK WHILE YOU REST

SABBATH

Then Jesus said to them, "The Sabbath was made to meet the needs of people, and not people to meet the requirements of the Sabbath."

Mark 2:27

How hard is it for you to stop working or to purposefully not do all the things on your to-do list?

What are some of the signs that your body is giving you to tell you it needs rest?

You know how important it is for your body to rest. I don't think I need to convince you that your body has limits and that when you push your body to operate beyond its limits it will eventually catch up to you. The problem isn't knowing that you need rest; it's believing that you can't have rest. There are two common reasons for why we believe that:

1. We think we can earn our blessings, so we stay busy.
2. We believe that our lives will fall apart if we aren't personally holding them together.

What are some of the reasons preventing you from taking one day a week to rest?

We think that the busier we are, the more value we bring, the better person we are, or the closer we are to securing what we want. However, God does not command us to always be busy. He does command us to rest.

The spiritual practice of Sabbath is learning how to stop living in constant motion so we can see where God is moving on our behalf. The bottom line for this spiritual practice is that you are blessed when you rest.

Overwhelm is an internal issue, but it can have physical consequences. In the *Stronger than Stress* book, I explain that our bodies interpret perceived threats (opening an unexpected bill or arguing with a loved one) the same as physical threats (a car accident or a burglary). Your body doesn't know the difference between an emotional threat and a mortal threat that puts your life in danger. Your body releases hormones created by God for specific, short-term, life-saving functions like jamming your foot on the gas pedal if you need to avoid a car accident. However, if you leave your foot on the gas pedal all the time, you're guaranteed at some point to crash or wear out your engine.

Sabbath is a spiritual practice that creates space away from the busyness for you to rest and connect with God. It also teaches your body to not react to every perceived threat. In my own life, this practice has lowered my stress levels over time.

Read Psalm 46:10 and write it in the space below. Underline the words "be still" and circle the phrase "know that I am God."

Stillness is productive because when we stop moving, we can see God and where He is working. We also practice undoing. Some of us are in the Energizer Bunny habit, and we need a weekly reminder that God doesn't need rest but we do. Also, if you're always moving and hustling, how can you observe what God is doing? Even more than that, how can you receive what God wants to give if you're forever in motion or always exhausted?

God never needs rest, but He is our first example of stopping and resting. In Genesis 2, after God finished creating the world in six days, He rested on the seventh day. God looked around and observed His creation. He gazed upon its goodness and appreciated it. This is what God wants for you as well. There's so much that God has done and is doing in your life, and He knows that you need to stop and notice it.

Why do you need to take time to stop and reflect on what God has done or to see what He is doing?

Read Mark 2:27 at the beginning of today's lesson. Underline why Sabbath was created. Write that reason in the space below.

What did Jesus mean when He said that the Sabbath was created to meet the needs of the people?

When Jesus taught about the Sabbath, He was speaking to religious leaders who had made the Sabbath about themselves. Even after the religious leaders added legalistic rules to the practice of Sabbath, that didn't take away from its God-given goodness. Jesus affirmed the Sabbath when He declared that it was made for us humans while simultaneously calling out the religious leaders for weighing down the day with traps and laws (Luke 6:1–11).

Are there any hang-ups or confusion that you have about practicing Sabbath?

What would it be like for you if there was one consistent day per week when you didn't have any appointments or obligations? What would you enjoy? What would be hard for you?

God didn't create you in His image to walk around this earth as a worn-out example of His people. Sabbath is an expression of grace! God gives us His goodness even though we don't earn it or deserve it.

Not only that, but when you are resting, there's a double bonus! As you learn that God can be trusted to take care of your life when you take a full day to rest your mind, body, and spirit, your trust in God overflows into the rest of your week. You stop pushing yourself because you're reminded that God can do more in an instant than you can do in a lifetime.

MEMORY VERSE MOMENT

How's this week's verse coming? Here's a chance to practice writing the first part of the verse:

_____ _____ ____ _____ ____ ____ _____

_____ _____ _____ ____—everything you heard from me and saw me doing. Then the peace of God will be with you.

Philippians 4:9

PRAYER

God, You are so good to give us rest. It's hard to stop when everything is always so busy. I pray for You to help me recognize that this is Your command for my life and that I can trust You when I'm resting. In Jesus's name, amen.

CREATING A SPIRITUAL PRACTICE OF SABBATH

They must realize that the Sabbath is the LORD's gift to you.

Exodus 16:29

Sabbath is a spiritual practice that reminds us of God's love and care for us as human beings, not human doings. An essential element of trusting God is to believe that He will show up for you, even when you aren't working.

Today's lesson is intended to be interactive, so if you aren't able to practice Sabbath today, use this lesson to plan your Sabbath experience—be intentional about scheduling a date on the calendar to put it into practice.

Read Exodus 16:29 above. How does God describe Sabbath?

God created Sabbath as a gift for you. This means you don't have to earn the right to rest. This also means that even if you have inescapable obligations, God can create a way for you to experience His gift. He isn't going to command Sabbath without providing ways for you to experience it.

As you allow yourself to experience the gift of Sabbath and just be, you'll also find grace in feeling time slow enough to push back on the busyness of life. Time stops for no one, but Sabbath holds within it a slowness that gives back to you in delightful ways. When there is nothing on your schedule and you have an entire day without needing to think about a to-do list or feeling pressure to compete, time slows in the most delicious of ways. You may not experience this at first as you're looking at the clock and thinking about what you could be doing. But the more you practice Sabbath, you'll come to experience the grace of slowing down time and the freedom from the hurry sickness that causes so much stress.

How do we practice Sabbath? What do we need to keep in mind? I like the Sabbath vision recorded by the prophet Isaiah:

> Keep the Sabbath day holy.
>> Don't pursue your own interests on that day,
> but enjoy the Sabbath
>> and speak of it with delight as the Lord's holy day.
> Honor the Sabbath in everything you do on that day,
>> and don't follow your own desires or talk idly. (Isa. 58:13)

What do you think that it means to keep the Sabbath day holy?

Notice the words "enjoy" and "delight." What do these words indicate about the attitude we should have toward practicing Sabbath?

Sabbath is God's weekly reminder for us that He is all we need. This brings us to the realization that we should celebrate on the Sabbath rather than worrying about what's not getting done or grumping over what we might be missing. When we practice letting God move while we don't, we discover that some of what we're rushing around to do doesn't need to get done. Some of those spinning plates can spin fine on their own without our obsessing about them. Sabbath is a practice that teaches us to let go of wrong beliefs and fears around needing to work too many hours or be involved with too many things.

As we see God taking care of our lives while we take care of ourselves, Sabbath becomes a practice that protects us from overloading our schedule.

Are you ready to put what you've learned into practice? Here are two different Sabbath practices you can choose from, or use both.

Sabbath Practice #1: Learn the Sabbath Rhythm

Rather than dictate specific, rigid rules about Sabbath, you can mimic the rhythm that God models for us when He finished creation. You can use this as a good preparation before you start your Sabbath:

> Then God looked over all he had made, and he saw that it was very good! (Gen. 1:31)

Here is that rhythm:

- **Look down.** Stop to reflect on and appreciate your hard work.
- **Look up.** Designate part of your Sabbath day to specifically give thanks to God and acknowledge your trust in Him as you rest for the day.
- **Rest to fill up.** Honor the Sabbath command by not only resting your body in a meaningful way, but also put your mind to rest by releasing the need to problem-solve or plan.
- **Repeat.** Make this a regular weekly practice.

Sabbath Practice #2: Planning Your Sabbath Using the Acronym ESPN

Why ESPN? I wanted to make it memorable so that you could share this with the people in your life. Here are four principles to help you home in and honor the Sabbath as God desires for you:

E—Enjoy Engaging with God and Others

Approach your practice of Sabbath with anticipation and joy. After all, it is a gift from God, not a trap to set you up for failure. Release your fears and concerns about certain scenarios to God. If He has gifted Sabbath to you, then He will reveal a solution.

S—Suspend Appointments and Obligations

This is the one day when you don't schedule anything on your calendar, nor do you plan for housework or errands. The goal is not only to keep your body from rushing around but also to let your mind rest.

Caring for children and loved ones doesn't break the Sabbath, but the care should not include running around to sports games and doctor appointments, doing chores, or problem-solving. This is a day for you to be present and invest in the people you love with your time and attention.

P—Plan Ahead

Be intentional about creating time with God to reflect on His goodness to you in the previous week. Plan whether you want to do this in prayer, by journaling, or on a walk.

Set yourself up for success by planning your meal the night before, cleaning up the parts of your home where you will spend your Sabbath, making plans to enjoy the day, and having a conversation with your family or loved ones about how to enjoy Sabbath together. Everyone will get excited if you explain that it's a rest day rather than a workday!

N—No Electronic Dependence

Devices aren't evil, but they can be a distraction and undermine the blessings that God wants you to experience on the Sabbath. A study conducted in 2017 revealed that the use of laptops by students in a classroom distracts everyone—not just the people using them![3]

Your devices can be used on the Sabbath if they don't interfere with the overall goal of making space for you to receive from God.

REFLECTION QUESTIONS

1. Based on today's study, how were you prompted to make your practice of Sabbath more intentional, or were you challenged in some other area?

2. As you review the practical applications, jot down some ideas that you have in the margin.

3. BONUS: Choose your Sabbath day and write it here:

_____

MEMORY VERSE MOMENT

Here we go! Write out this week's memory verse in the space below.

PRAYER

God, thank You for the gift of Sabbath rest. I can trust that Your faithfulness, power, and love will be in charge of my life while I recharge. In Jesus's name, amen.

De-Stressing Your Thoughts

Prayer
Engaging Scripture

MEMORY VERSE

The Lord gives his people strength.
The Lord blesses them with peace.

Psalm 29:11

OVERCOMING OOPS THINKING

And now, dear brothers and sisters, one final thing. Fix your thoughts on what is true, and honorable, and right, and pure, and lovely, and admirable. Think about things that are excellent and worthy of praise.

Philippians 4:8

A study published in 2020 estimates that the average human has over six thousand thoughts per day.[1] Our minds are a constant spin of who, what, when, where, why, and how.

I don't know about you, but I think about stuff that I'm not actually conscious I'm thinking about. For example, I once drove across a whole state replaying an entire relationship with someone in my mind—what went right, what went wrong, and everything in between. I'd driven about 150 miles before I realized how engrossed I was in my own thoughts.

One of the yellow flags that statistic sparked for me was the caution that if we aren't aware of the thoughts we have, then we may be building thought pathways to destinations that are detrimental to our mental health or our faith. Here's a little exercise that gives you a chance to think about your thinking:

Fill in the blanks with what you think about in each setting. Then circle if your thoughts tend to be positive, negative, or a mix of both.

At home:	Positive	Negative	Both
Driving:	Positive	Negative	Both

Paying bills:	Positive	Negative	Both
Eating:	Positive	Negative	Both
At church:	Positive	Negative	Both
Working:	Positive	Negative	Both
Other:	Positive	Negative	Both

As humans, we lean toward the negative, even when it's something small. Psychologist Rick Hanson observes, "The mind is like Velcro for negative experiences and Teflon for positive ones."[2] This is known as negative bias.

In my life, I like to call this OOPS thinking. Here's what I mean by that:

- **Overthinking.** Pondering a problem or situation too long or considering it too much.
- **Obsessing.** A laser-lock focus on a situation that warps your perspective on the rest of your life.
- **Panicking.** An emotional, out-of-control reaction to a situation with little ability to apply wisdom or discernment.
- **Supersizing.** Looking for ways to make an ordinary or difficult problem bigger.

What's interesting to me is that I don't have to coach myself toward negative thoughts. It doesn't take effort for me to overthink. I don't have to try hard to make it happen. Obsessing is way easier than I want it to be.

Which OOPS behaviors are familiar to you?

In today's lesson, Paul provides a remedy for OOPS thinking. Let's be honest, life is already tough, and when we add negative thinking on top of life's challenges, we're weighing ourselves down even more.

If you've been around people who are OOPS thinkers, they do not weather life's challenges well. It's easy to fall into the OOPS trap, so if you're there, today's study offers a path that guides you toward God's freedom. You can focus on replacing your OOPS thoughts with Scripture-directed thoughts.

At the beginning of today's study, you noted what you think about at various points throughout your day. Now, let's incorporate Philippians 4:8 to reshape your thoughts by using Scripture.

First, select an attribute to write beside each of the activities listed in the first column. Then, using that attribute, write out a Scripture-directed thought in the right column. An example has been provided for you.

ATTRIBUTES

True	Lovely
Honorable	Admirable
Right	Worthy of praise
Pure	

Activity	Attribute	Scripture-directed thought
At home		
Driving		
Paying bills	Right	*God will provide. I'll praise Him for it now.*
Eating		
At church		
Working		
Other		

Why does Paul instruct believers to pursue these types of thoughts?

In 1 Corinthians 2:10–16, Paul teaches that as we receive the truths of God's Spirit, we develop the mind of Christ. The attributes in Philippians 4:8 reflect the mind of Christ. Even as Jesus contended with stress and countless problems, He kept His thoughts from becoming sour and negative.

Just for today, pay attention to the kinds of thoughts that you have, especially when you're under stress. What do your thoughts tell you about yourself?

What is a takeaway, a unique insight, or an aha moment from today's study that you'd like to remember?

MEMORY VERSE MOMENT

Write out this week's memory verse in the space below.

PRAYER

God, I confess the thoughts that I have don't always reflect my faith or trust in You. As I shift my thinking back toward putting You at the center, I welcome Your peace into my life. In Jesus's name, amen.

TALKING AND LISTENING TO GOD

PRAYER

So let us come boldly to the throne of our gracious God. There we will receive his mercy, and we will find grace to help us when we need it most.

Hebrews 4:16

While practicing surrender provides a space for us to let go of what we can't control in exchange for God's peace, the spiritual practice of prayer is how we learn the language of God and how He communicates with us.

Based on my experience serving on a large church staff and traveling around the country as an author, prayer is one of the areas of the Christian life that many are uncomfortable engaging in. Common insecurities around prayer include wondering if there is a right way and a wrong way to pray, feeling unsure about what to say, comparing our prayers to the prayers of others, and questioning how long a prayer needs to be. It all comes down to the big question that many people ask: *How can I pray in such a way that God will answer my prayer?*

There are a lot of teachings on prayer and how it works. In today's lesson we will cover four principles for establishing a practice of prayer.

What are lingering questions, confusion, or frustrations that you have with prayer?

How would you describe your current prayer habit?

God knows that He is the safest place on the planet for you. The Scriptures tell us that God is our refuge, our fortress. We are safe to share our fears and our desires in prayer, and God gives us the security of His promises and His faithfulness.

Not only that, God holds an abundance to give: His peace, power, provision, character, unconditional love, wisdom, and purpose. If you were in God's place, wouldn't you long to share that with humanity? Wouldn't you want your people to come to you to receive it? Prayer is how we receive.

Four Prayer Principles

1. Prayer is about centering our attention on God, not us.

When Jesus teaches His followers how to pray in Matthew 6, He puts God at the center, which is a practice that we should follow for effective prayer. Our motivation for praying is to know God. Our desire to pray arises from our need to connect with God.

As a Pharisee, Paul would have grown up praying a lot. One of the classic prayers that Paul would have prayed and that Jewish people still pray today is the Shema:

> Listen, O Israel! The LORD is our God, the LORD alone. And you must love the LORD your God with all your heart, all your soul, and all your strength. (Deut. 6:4–5)

What is the difference between centering on God in your prayers versus praying only for yourself or others?

In Mark 12:29–31, Jesus quoted the Shema to teach that loving God is an act of obedience, which contrasted with the teaching of the Jewish religious leaders who said it is an obligation. Jesus taught from the foundation of grace, so the Shema became less about rules and more about a relationship with God. Believers turn their hearts toward God and He fills them with Himself.

2. Prayer values relationship, not rules.

Over the years, I've heard from countless individuals who grew up in religious traditions with strict rules about prayer—who was allowed to pray, what had to be said, or where prayer could take place. Sadly, prayer has been the source of stress for many Christians.

Read Matthew 6:9. Jesus teaches us to pray starting with a specific name of God. What is it?

Our earthly fathers aren't always perfect, loving, or present, but God is. God loves it when you talk to Him without worrying about using fancy words or making a mistake. Prayer is not a graded test, nor is prayer a talent contest. When you get to heaven, no one will receive a trophy for the longest, fanciest, or most moving prayer.

3. Prayer realigns our desires with God's.

There's nothing wrong with making requests to God in prayer. But as Elisabeth Elliot describes, "Prayer lays hold of God's plan and becomes the link between his will and its accomplishment on earth. Amazing things happen, and we are given the privilege of being the channels of the Holy Spirit's prayer."[3]

Read Matthew 6:10. Where does Jesus instruct us to pray for God's will to be done?

Prayer reminds us of God's eternal plan for humanity. Each time you pray and center God in your prayer, you're reminded that life is more than what is happening in the moment. You're reminded of God's promises, His character, His faithfulness, but also His priorities. God has called us to become like Christ, to live by the Holy Spirit, and to shine our light of hope as Christ's ambassadors.

4. Prayer offers us a place to come for mercy and grace.

If you've been wondering when I'll finally talk about prayer as the place where we make our requests to God, it's now. Yes, God invites us to make our requests known to Him (Phil. 4:6–7). God cares about all the details of our lives, both big and small.

Prayer gives us a life-giving action step when we are overwhelmed by any circumstance or situation.

Reread Hebrews 4:16 at the beginning of today's lesson. What are the two words that describe how you can approach God in prayer?

Tomorrow, I'll share two prayer tools that you can use to begin a prayer practice or add to your existing prayer practice.

For those who were never taught to pray or have been hesitant to pray, I have a special word of encouragement for you: Go for it! God wants to hear from you, especially if you've been struggling.

MEMORY VERSE MOMENT

Fill in the blanks for this week's memory verse:

The LORD gives his people _____.

The LORD blesses them with _____.

Psalm 29:11

PRAYER

God, thank You for the means to connect with You in prayer. I love that even though You don't need my prayers, You desire them because You want me to know You. Draw me close to You so that I know You more. In Jesus's name, amen.

CREATING A SPIRITUAL PRACTICE OF PRAYER

The spiritual practice of prayer is the cord that connects us to God's love and strength. The more that we meet God in prayer, the more opportunities we have to receive the reality and reassurance of God's love.

In my life, it has taken decades for prayer to become my default. When I'm stressed, my survival mode reaction is to fight or try to fix things. Settling down into prayer caused anxiety because I didn't trust what God would do. Even though I knew that prayer was helpful, I put my trust in helping myself . . . which usually ended up making a mess.

The aha moment for me happened when I realized that God is the safest person in the world. When I centered God in my prayers and took time to enlarge my view of God beyond my stress and my problems, my stress and my problems shrunk down. That's when I shifted my mindset toward praying first and then being patient before acting. A total game changer.

In today's lesson, you'll learn two practical application tools to equip you in establishing or refreshing your prayer practice. This lesson is interactive, so use this study time to engage in the practices and reflect on them at the end of the lesson.

Practical Application #1: PRAY Method

There are many helpful methods to assist you in establishing a practice of prayer. The PRAY method is a simple framework that incorporates the principles you learned in yesterday's lesson. You can follow this method by praying aloud or writing out your prayer in the space below.

P—*Praise*

Begin with centering on God by remembering Who He is, His eternal plan, and His faithfulness.

R—*Repent*

Tell God about your struggles, sin, and anything else on your heart. Ask for forgiveness and for God's help to turn toward God and away from wrong attitudes or behaviors.

A—*Ask*

Make your requests known to God. Tell Him about everything, big and small.

Y—*"Yes, God"*

Yield to God's sovereignty and eternal plan. This is where you follow Jesus's example of praying "I want your will to be done, not mine." Affirm that you trust God no matter what happens.

Practical Application #2: Establishing a Prayer Rhythm for Your Life

Daily—Spend intentional time with God each day using the PRAY method.

Spend the amount of time that you'd want to spend with someone who means a lot to you. Keep that conversation going throughout the day.

Weekly—Write out your prayers in a journal once or more per week.

This is helpful for the seasons of life when you feel lost, overwhelmed, or disconnected from God. You can see your life with God on paper and be encouraged.

Monthly—Meet with a friend to pray.

Throughout Scripture, we see countless examples of believers praying together. Praying with others is an important part of your prayer practice. You can meet online, in the carpool line, in the grocery store parking lot, or at the park. Spend ten minutes checking in with each other and then each of you can pray.

Annually—Get away for a weekend prayer retreat.

Just as Jesus took time away from His busy schedule to rest and talk with God, you can too! There might be religious communities in your area that will rent you a small cabin or hermitage. The great part is that you won't need to pack much since it's a prayer retreat. Bring your Bible, a journal, a worship playlist (downloaded since Wi-Fi might be unavailable), and comfy walking clothes and shoes.

REFLECTION QUESTIONS

1. What are your takeaways from engaging in the practice of prayer?

2. Did you sense a connection or response from God? What was it?

3. Are there any adjustments you could make so that this practice would be more meaningful and sustainable for you?

MEMORY VERSE MOMENT

Fill in the blanks for this week's memory verse:

The Lord _____ _____ _____ _____.

The Lord _____ _____ _____ _____.

Psalm 29:11

PRAYER

God, thank You for creating prayer as a way for me to know You. I'm grateful that You desire for me to understand the depth and fullness of Your love for me. As I consider these prayer practices, help me commit to regular, relational time with You so that I can know You more and live more fully for You. In Jesus's name, amen.

ENGAGING WITH GOD'S WORD

SCRIPTURE

All Scripture is inspired by God and is useful to teach us what is true and to make us realize what is wrong in our lives. It corrects us when we are wrong and teaches us to do what is right. God uses it to prepare and equip his people to do every good work.

2 Timothy 3:16–17

In our modern times, we have access to new solutions, technologies, ways of thinking, and possibilities. However, not every idea or solution leads us down healthy, helpful, or holy paths.

These days, we've confused information for power, wisdom, and even more dangerously, truth. While information can improve lives, save lives, and even bring people together, having access at our fingertips to all the world's knowledge cannot heal our deepest wounds, transform our spirits, or save our souls.

When it comes to reading Scripture, the problem isn't that we don't have the information. We've allowed the urgency of our lives to push aside the importance of choosing God's Word as the primary search engine for how to live.

Read 2 Timothy 3:16–17 above. Fill in the blanks on the four roles of Scripture in your life. (For answers, see the bottom of page 96.)

1. Scripture teaches you what is _____.

2. Scripture awakens you to what is _____.

3. Scripture _____ you with God's new direction.

4. Scripture _____ you to do what is right.

In 2022, the American Bible Society reported that 26 million Americans had stopped or almost completely stopped reading their Bibles over the course of the previous year. One year! Lead researcher John Plake admits their team was shocked. "We reviewed our calculations. We double-checked our math and ran the numbers again . . . and again. What we discovered was startling, disheartening, and disruptive."[4]

There is a strong spirit of confusion in our world today. Long ago, Paul explained why:

> For a time is coming when people will no longer listen to sound and wholesome teaching. They will follow their own desires and will look for teachers who will tell them whatever their itching ears want to hear. (2 Tim. 4:3)

How do you see 2 Timothy 4:3 reflected in our culture today?

Why do you think that people have itching ears and no longer want the life-giving power of God's Word in their lives?

Tomorrow, you'll learn spiritual practices that will help you to engage more with the Bible in your life. I use the word "engage" intentionally

Answers: 1. true 2. wrong 3. corrects 4. teaches

because the spiritual practice of Scripture is more than reading your Bible. It's about finding ways to incorporate God's Word into every area of your heart, mind, actions, and life. If you read your Bible, close it, and don't think about it the rest of the day, you'll miss out on experiencing the God-breathed power of the Scriptures. Imagine getting out an electric mixer to blend cake batter, but after you plug it in, you never flip on the power switch. You'd still be able to mix the cake, but not in the same way that electric power provides. Some people think that the Bible offers good advice but sadly miss out on its life-transforming power.

> For the word of God is alive and powerful. It is sharper than the sharpest two-edged sword, cutting between soul and spirit, between joint and marrow. It exposes our innermost thoughts and desires. (Heb. 4:12)

What does the Bible do inside of you?

How does Hebrews 4:12 refute the claims people make that the Bible is an old and irrelevant book?

Reflect on your experience with the Bible. What are some of the things you've learned that have changed your life or transformed how you live?

The power of God's Word has a way of slicing through confusion, mixed motives, denial, blind spots, and sin to show us the truth that can set us free (John 8:32). While skeptics and critics continue to question the inerrancy (i.e., without error) of Scripture, the Bible is the most scrutinized, debated, researched, and referenced work in human history. It continues to stand the test of time because it continues to transform lives. "God uses the Word to enable us to see the sin and unbelief in our own hearts. The Word exposes our hearts, and then, if we trust God, the Word enables our hearts to obey God and claim his promises."[5]

In tomorrow's lesson, you'll learn some practical ways to engage Scripture so that you can create or refresh this spiritual practice in your life.

What is an aha moment or takeaway that you want to remember from today's lesson?

MEMORY VERSE MOMENT

Fill in the blanks for this week's memory verse:

The LORD gives his people strength.

_____ _____ _____ _____

_____ _____.

Psalm 29:11

PRAYER

God, thank You for giving me Your Word to teach, lead, and guide me through this confusing life. I desire to experience the living and active power of Your Word. Open my eyes to understand Scripture more and incorporate it into every area of my life. In Jesus's name, amen.

CREATING A SPIRITUAL PRACTICE OF ENGAGING SCRIPTURE

But Jesus told him, "No! The Scriptures say, 'People do not live by bread alone, but by every word that comes from the mouth of God.'"

Matthew 4:4

When Jesus was in the wilderness, hungry and pressured by Satan to fall into temptation, He relied on Scripture to sustain Him. Jesus spoke from Deuteronomy, reminding us that for every hunger we have in life—whether a hunger for peace, less stress, or less overwhelm—making space for engaging Scripture will sustain us in a life-giving way. Any human substitutes will leave us starving.

How can you give the Bible a higher priority in your life? Today's interactive lesson is intended to help you establish a life-giving practice of reading Scripture without feeling like it's one more thing on your overwhelming to-do list.

Read Psalm 1:2–3. What is the attitude of the person who reads God's Word?

The Hebrew word translated as "delight" in most English Bibles is *chephets* (pronounced *khay-phets*), which means "to desire or find pleasure in."[6] Notice the consequences of their delight: God's Word sustains them no matter their circumstances or season of life.

What do you think contributes to a person delighting in Scripture?

Look again at Psalm 1:2. What does the person who delights in God's Word do day and night? How does their pleasure translate to their practice?

For us to delight or find pleasure in something, we first need to experience it. If someone puts a new dessert in front of me, I won't delight in it until I've tasted it and experienced the pleasure of its flavor for myself. The psalmist points out that those who delight in God's Word have experienced its pleasure in their lives and thrive no matter the season they are in.

List two or three reasons why you read your Bible.

Identify times when you enjoy reading your Bible. Is it in a specific place, with certain people, at a specific time?

Other than reading your Bible, what are other ways that you've enjoyed interacting with God's Word?

Your practice of engaging with Scripture isn't about sitting in a chair for a certain amount of time. This practice is about giving yourself the chance to read, ponder, memorize, write out, and recite God's Word throughout the day.

Practicing Engaging with Scripture and Meditation

Pick one or two of the following ideas to try after today's lesson.

1. Write out Scripture verses and tape them to your bathroom mirror or other places where you'll read them.
2. Listen to an audio Bible when you're in the car, at the gym, or at night before bed.
3. Read Bible verses with family or friends at mealtimes, over coffee, or before bed, and discuss the Scriptures together.
4. Memorize Bible verses that reflect an area of your life in which you believe God wants to change your heart.
5. Sing! Lots of classic hymns and modern worship songs incorporate Scripture. Find those songs. As you sing, you're engaging with God's Word and worshiping Him too.
6. Use Bible dictionaries, commentaries, and online resources to help you better understand Scripture. Tools such as Logos Bible Software and Biblegateway.com offer great connections to resources.
7. Sign up for an online platform that will email you a Bible verse or Bible study content each morning.
8. If you sign up for a Bible-in-a-year plan or a guided Bible study like this one, give yourself permission to establish a goal of regular engagement but do not judge your performance by how closely you follow their established timetable. Prioritize commitment, not completion of a specific schedule.
9. Pick one Bible verse from your church's weekly sermon and journal about what the verse taught you about God and how you can apply it to your life.

10. If you'd like a simple framework for doing your own Bible study without a guided Bible study experience like this one, you can use the SOAP method outlined below.

SOAP Study Method

This is a basic framework that equips you to study the Bible on your own. I've included a verse on the next page if you'd like to try this out. I've used the SOAP method for over fifteen years and it's a format that allows you to be as simple or in-depth as you'd like with Scripture.

S—Scripture. Choose a passage of Scripture, whether from a daily reading plan, a devotional, or YouVersion's verse of the day. Take your time reading and allow God to speak to you. When you are done, look for a verse that particularly spoke to you that day and write it in your journal.

O—Observation. What do you think God is saying to you in this passage? Ask the Holy Spirit to teach you and reveal Jesus to you. Paraphrase this Scripture in your own words and write it down in your journal.

A—Application. Personalize what you have read by asking yourself how it applies to your life right now. Perhaps it is instruction, encouragement, revelation of a new promise, or correction for a particular area of your life. Write how this passage can apply to you today.

P—Prayer. This can be as simple as asking God to help you use this passage, or it may be a greater insight on what He may be revealing to you. Remember, prayer is a two-way conversation, so be sure to listen to what God has to say! Now, write it out.

Here's a verse you can use to test out the SOAP method. If you'd like to make sure that you're on the right track, go to BarbRoose.com/SOAP for an example of how this can look fully completed and to access a thirty-day SOAP Scripture list.

> And now, dear brothers and sisters, one final thing. Fix your thoughts on what is true, and honorable, and right, and pure, and lovely, and admirable. Think about things that are excellent and worthy of praise. (Phil. 4:8)

S—Scripture

O—Observation

A—Application

P—Prayer

REFLECTION QUESTIONS

1. What can a regular spiritual practice of engaging with Scripture do in your life that you aren't currently experiencing?

2. How does the idea of engaging with Scripture in a variety of ways differ from the standard presentation of sitting with one's Bible in a chair for a set period of time?

3. Did you sense a connection or response from God? What was it?

4. Are there any adjustments that you could make so that this practice would be more meaningful and sustainable for you?

MEMORY VERSE MOMENT

It's the end of the week and time for you to write out this week's memory verse. You can do it!

PRAYER

God, Your Word gives me life! I want to experience the delight of studying Your Word. Make me willing where I'm not. In Jesus's name, amen.

Bringing God's Peace to Stressful Places

Simplicity • Self-Care

MEMORY VERSE

Not that I was ever in need, for I have learned how to be content with whatever I have.

Philippians 4:11

GOD, AM I DOING SOMETHING WRONG?

Why do we hold on to the belief that if God calls us to something, then the journey should be stress-free? Whether we sense God calling us to start a ministry, take a job, buy a house, foster a child, move to a different community, or attend a certain church, there is an expectation that if we pray about it in advance, plan effectively, and even save all the money, we're setting ourselves up for guaranteed success. Some of us may take a few extra spiritual steps by adding in some fasting, anointing with oil, and laying on of hands. These are all good things, but they are no guarantee that we will never face big problems or stress. Yet, how often do we treat them that way?

You might be thinking about all the problems that you're facing in your life today and wondering if you're doing something wrong. Put a pin in that thought as you look at today's lesson.

For a guy who was highly committed to Jesus, Paul seemed to be a magnet for problems.

> When we arrived in Macedonia, there was no rest for us. We faced conflict from every direction, with battles on the outside and fear on the inside. (2 Cor. 7:5)

There are certain Christians today who believe that a lack of problems is a sign of God's favor. There are other Christians who believe (or fear) that prolonged periods of hardship or difficulty are a sign of God's anger or disappointment. Those perspectives conflict with Jesus's teaching in John 16:33. God's favor is a good thing! It's a divine means of help as we navigate life's situations so that we can live out the gospel and tell of God's glory. Problem-free shouldn't be the goal of our Christian life or anything that we pursue. As we learn about Paul's life, pay attention to how often God's favor shows up in Paul's circumstances. Beyond carrying Paul through those difficulties, God's favor enabled Paul and others to experience miraculous moments.

How does it feel when you're caught up in problems that you didn't cause and you're feeling the stress because other people are stirring up trouble?

When it rains, it pours.

That's how Paul and his traveling companion, Silas, must have felt in Acts 16. After sensing the Holy Spirit was blocking them from their original plan to preach in Asia, and after a man appeared to Paul in a vision telling him to come to Macedonia, the two men headed for the city of Philippi (vv. 1–12). Bible scholars refer to this as the Macedonian Call.

You'd think that after the Holy Spirit blocked Paul from going in one direction and God sent a vision telling him to go in a different direction, then good things for the gospel would be waiting for Paul and Silas when they arrived. Not quite. Things started off well in verses 13–15 as Paul met a group of women who had gathered to pray, including an influential woman named Lydia. Paul baptized Lydia's family and she hosted the two men in her home. Then things took a turn.

Read Acts 16:16–24. List the problems that Paul and Silas encountered.

Paul wasn't looking for trouble, but the young fortune teller in Acts 16 bounced on Paul's last nerve until he finally called the evil spirit out of the girl. This should have been a good thing, but Paul's action invited a new set of problems because her handlers could no longer exploit the girl for money. That girl had been their golden ticket, but no more.

Picture the scene in your mind as the girl's masters grabbed Paul and Silas and dragged them to the authorities. They accused Paul and Silas of instigating public unrest, even though they had done nothing of the sort. Of course, once they started yelling and people began gathering, then there was a public problem. That's when Paul and Silas were beaten before being tossed into prison. None of that was fair to Paul and Silas.

Yet, as we will see, how Paul and Silas handled their situation was inspiring, and God showed up in a miraculous way.

Read the following verses and record your answers in the space provided.

Acts 16:25–26
What were Paul and Silas doing in prison? What happened around midnight, and how did that affect Paul and Silas?

Acts 16:27–28

Why was the jailer about to kill himself? Why didn't he?

Acts 16:29–30

What did the jailer ask Paul and Silas? Why do you think he asked that question?

Acts 16:31–34

How was the jailer's life transformed because of Paul and Silas being in prison? How did he care for Paul and Silas?

We must not minimize the difficulties that Paul and Silas experienced, such as the false accusations by the girl's masters, the beatings, and their imprisonment. But the fact that they praised God instead of fixating on their stress and pain is something for us to pay attention to. Even though the two men could have been discouraged when they ran into such difficult people despite their obedience to God, Paul and Silas continued to praise God and saw Him move in miraculous ways.

Read Psalm 34:19. How often does a godly person run into struggles? What does God do in response?

Why shouldn't we assume that another believer has done something wrong if they run into hardship or difficulty in their lives?

I hope that reading this story from Paul's life encourages you to remember that we all have problems, even those of us who've been Christians for a long time. God is with you through them all!

MEMORY VERSE MOMENT

Read through the memory verse at the start of the lesson and underline the words that are meaningful to you.

PRAYER

God, thank You for Paul and Silas's example of how to continue praising You, even when there are problems that pop up everywhere. Help me to remember that, no matter how many problems I face, You will never fail me at any time. In Jesus's name, amen.

DECLUTTERING THE YESES

SIMPLICITY

So don't worry about these things, saying, "What will we eat? What will we drink? What will we wear?" These things dominate the thoughts of unbelievers, but your heavenly Father already knows all your needs. Seek the Kingdom of God above all else, and live righteously, and he will give you everything you need.

Matthew 6:31–33

In a *Huffington Post* survey, 84 percent of respondents admitted they have too much stuff. Over half of those respondents believed that their stuff caused them a lot of stress. They also felt like their inability to organize, clean, and find household items when needed was the source of rising stress.[1]

I don't have too much stuff, but I do own way too many pairs of jeans. In my hopes of finding that one elusive pair that makes me look taller, thinner, and curvier, I own jeans in every type of light, medium, and dark wash. I keep buying and hoping. And bless it, a new pair was delivered yesterday . . .

What do you own too much of?

What do you continue to buy even though you already have enough?

How much of your daily overwhelm do you contribute to having too much to organize or keep track of?

Today, we're going to talk about stuff. More specifically, we're going to look at what Jesus has to say about our stuff. We'll then explore simplicity as a spiritual practice so you learn how to identify and intentionally focus on the main thing, and find contentment in all things.

Before we go further, however, it's important to recognize that simplicity is not about stripping your life of all possessions or limiting yourself to owning one cup, one plate, and one pair of shoes.

Simplicity begins with clarity amid all of life's choices.

Read Matthew 6:31–33 and complete the following:

List what you aren't supposed to worry about:	List what you are to focus on first:

What will God give you when you put Him first? What does that mean?

Jesus says to focus on the main thing: God. By first seeking His kingdom and His righteousness, you will be led by His wisdom and eternal plan, and the guidance of the Holy Spirit will equip you to make wiser decisions. Are you familiar with the illustration of fitting large rocks and sand into a jar? If you pour in the sand and then drop in the rocks, there won't be enough room. However, if you begin with the big rocks, then pour in the sand, everything will fit. This is the same with God. His Word and His way are the biggest priorities in your life. As you see life God's way, that will inform your daily choices and help you discern difficult problems.

You might be wondering how to tie Jesus's command to the daily choices that you need to make. For sure, there are choices that will require prayer, discernment, and wisdom. However, there are many choices that we can eliminate during the day to focus more on loving God, which will bring us more peace than anything else.

You may already know this but it's worth saying again: the more that you have, the more decisions you need to make. Decision fatigue can lead to overwhelm if you feel like you can't keep up with all the decisions. The more decisions we must make, the more our brain needs to work, and that work tires us out.

It has been estimated that the average person needs to make 35,000 decisions per day.[2] It's not so much about the number of decisions you have to make but the weight of each decision and the potential impact it will have on your life and the lives of those you care about. Deciding between two types of salsa is one thing. Processing constant decisions about a loved one's mental health care or financial decisions when you're on the brink of financial collapse is quite another.

This brings us to an important lesson that Paul learned in his life.

Read Philippians 4:11–13. What word describes the attitude that Paul learned to develop? List the conditions in which Paul learned to be content.

How does Paul's contentment translate to his life experience? (v. 13)

Where in your life can you identify a lack of contentment and things that you've committed to or purchased to make up for that lack of contentment?

Paul's perspective on contentment is that God is all he needs. Period. From that posture, Paul allowed every possession and opportunity to flow through his open hands without getting attached to it. In prison, Paul was permitted to have others provide for his needs, but it's not likely he had a full fridge, complete bedroom set, or sectional sofa. He was likely chained to the wall or floor, yet what little Paul had was enough.

Tomorrow's lesson will feature insights into Paul's journey to learn contentment. Notice how it was something that he had to understand for himself, which means there was a point in his life when Paul may not have embraced contentment. If you can relate, the good news is that you also can learn contentment or increase your contentment. The payoff is strength to face all circumstances and live out your faith. It's not easy, but it's worth it!

MEMORY VERSE MOMENT

Fill in the blanks:

Not that I was ever in need, for I have _____ _____ _____

____ _____ with whatever I have.

Philippians 4:11

PRAYER

God, I want to put You first in my life so that I don't drown myself in a sea of overwhelming daily decisions. I want to live out Your priorities so that I can embrace simplicity, walk in Your purpose for me, and experience Your peace. In Jesus's name, amen.

CREATING A SPIRITUAL PRACTICE OF SIMPLICITY

In our world today, simplicity is a hard sell. The notion of choosing less so you can live more might raise some eyebrows. Richard Foster notes that "of all of the disciplines [practices] simplicity is the most visible."[3] Practicing simplicity doesn't mean that you need to sell your home or belongings. However, it may lead you to realize that your stuff is making it hard for you to worship God.

In yesterday's lesson, we learned that simplicity is a spiritual practice that involves knowing how to identify the main thing, being intentional to focus on the main thing, and finding contentment in all things.

Today, we'll learn how to put this into practice. As part of this interactive lesson, you can choose one of the practical suggestions at the end of the lesson and experiment with this practice today.

Jesus offers guidance for us with regard to practicing simplicity:

Don't store up treasures here on earth, where moths eat them and rust destroys them, and where thieves break in and steal. Store your treasures in heaven, where moths and rust cannot destroy, and thieves do not break in and steal. Wherever your treasure is, there the desires of your heart will also be. (Matt. 6:19–21)

What is the principle that Jesus wants you to understand about the power of your possessions over your heart?

Many Christians give this passage a wink and a smile because we compare our lives to the excess of mainstream culture and give ourselves a pass. However, Jesus is speaking to all of us. Our treasure is anything that we value above other things. Treasures can easily become idols, whether it's a home, a car, clothes, shoes, collections, purses. One of the questions that I've asked myself is, "If that item was taken away tomorrow, would I be angry with God for letting it be taken away?" Of course, if a home burns down or an heirloom is stolen, there would be natural grief and anger that a tragedy has happened. My question is a question of the heart. If we center our self-esteem, image, or ability to cope on some *thing*, then that item has control over our heart. The danger is that "we can become shackled by the material things of life, but we ought to be liberated and controlled by the Spirit of God."[4]

List possessions that you need to prayerfully discern whether to have present in your life.

For over twenty years I lived in a five-bedroom historical home that was built in 1905. When I went through my divorce, I was tempted to keep my house even though my kids were all adults. However, I decided to let go of the house. Owning a historical home means unexpected repairs and expensive remodeling, and I didn't want to live in a big house alone. Upon reflection, I realized my desire to keep the house was to push back against some of the shame of going through a divorce and to have something tangible to show for such a large part of my life. I had to surrender all of that to God because keeping the house wasn't going to heal my heart—only God could do that.

List any possessions you are holding on to because of emotional attachment, to increase your self-esteem, to prove your self-worth, or to soothe yourself for unfulfilled dreams.

Each of us must prayerfully discern how to live out the practice of simplicity. The goal of this practice is to be content with what God has provided and not overwhelm yourself with stuff that won't pass the test of eternity. Simplicity is living in the freedom and knowledge that God is enough for whatever you will ever need.

Principles for Establishing a Practice of Simplicity

1. **Prioritize loving God and others.** Determine what is getting in the way of your relationship with God or spending quality time with others.
2. **Investigate discontentment.** If there is an area in which you feel longing or dissatisfaction—whether it is about where you live, the car you drive, the income you make, or another area— invite God into that part of your life to move your heart toward contentment.
3. **Define your simplicity.** What types of decisions are draining you each day? How could you reduce the number of decisions

you have to make? If you made fewer decisions, how would that simplicity ease the overwhelm or stress in your life?

4. **Cap your collection.** Determine now how much of any one hobby or collection you will keep. Develop a system to donate or sell items as you acquire new pieces.

5. **Ask simplicity questions.**

   - Am I able to sufficiently address the other obligations in my life before I add this to my schedule or take on this responsibility?

   - Will this decision or purchase increase my energy or time to love others, or will it take away from my energy and time?

   - Am I buying this because I'm trying to please someone else, live up to a certain expectation, raise my self-esteem, or reduce my guilt?

   - Do I have to buy or say yes to this now, or could I postpone the decision and revisit it six months from now?

Practical Ideas to Move toward Simplicity

1. Create a capsule wardrobe that consists of five shirts, five pairs of pants, five layering pieces (e.g., sweaters, blazers, vests), five pairs of shoes, and five dresses. (You can also create a capsule wardrobe for your kids.)

2. Establish a maximum number of certain household items that tend to get out of control; for example, brands of cereal, hair-care products, streaming subscriptions, televisions.

3. Agree on three brands of products your family will use. You can switch out those brands in a family meeting every six months or annually.

4. Create and alternate two weekly menus to simplify shopping and dinner choices.

5. Institute a one-year fast from purchasing things that you already have too much of; for example, body lotions, certain clothing items, supplies for crafting or other hobbies.

6. Before busy months like May and December, predetermine the number of parties or special events that you will attend.

7. Implement a "get one, give one" policy in your home. For every new item that is purchased, a similar item should be donated.

8. Once a month, eliminate or donate the number of items equivalent to the days of the month.

REFLECTION QUESTIONS

1. What are your takeaways from engaging in this practice?

2. Did you sense a connection or response from God? What was it?

3. Are there any adjustments that you could make so that this practice would be more meaningful and sustainable for you?

MEMORY VERSE MOMENT

Fill in the blanks for the memory verse as you continue to work on memorizing it.

Not that I was _____ _____ _____, for I have learned how to be content with _____ ___ _____.

Philippians 4:11

PRAYER

God, I need Your wisdom to help me discern what simplicity looks like for me in this season of my life. I am open to be guided by Your Spirit in whatever You are calling me to keep, let go of, or give away. You have permission to clear away the clutter in my life so that I trust and depend only on You. In Jesus's name, amen.

TAKING CARE OF YOU

SELF-CARE

Then he [Elijah] went on alone into the wilderness, traveling all day. He sat down under a solitary broom tree and prayed that he might die. "I have had enough, LORD," he said. "Take my life, for I am no better than my ancestors who have already died."

Then he lay down and slept under the broom tree. But as he was sleeping, an angel touched him and told him, "Get up and eat!" He looked around and there beside his head was some bread baked on hot stones and a jar of water! So he ate and drank and lay down again.

Then the angel of the LORD came again and touched him and said, "Get up and eat some more, or the journey ahead will be too much for you."

1 Kings 19:4–7

What do Elijah's words in this passage reveal about his state of mind?

What are the angel's instructions to Elijah?

After defeating the false prophets of Baal at Mount Carmel, Elijah hustled out of there, especially after Israel's queen, Jezebel, put a bounty on his head. Instead of celebrating such a triumphant moment, Elijah felt defeated. He despaired so much that he wanted to die. He had faced down hundreds of false prophets, spending all day in that intense situation, and had also spent physical labor in building an altar and letting God use him in a magnificent supernatural showdown. Anyone would be tired after that. But being tired plus having your enemies chasing you? Well, that's overwhelming.

Elijah was so worn out that he went to sleep under a tree. God sent an angel to make sure that Elijah ate something, so he did. But Elijah was so exhausted that he didn't jump right back on the road. He went back to sleep instead of pushing himself to continue. This is self-care.

When you are overwhelmed, do you tend to take better care of yourself or neglect yourself?

What are some of the physical, emotional, or mental signs that you aren't taking care of yourself as well as you should?

It's rare to run into a woman who doesn't believe in self-care, but ask Christian women if self-care is a worthy discipleship conversation and the opinions can be strong and varied. Some believe that the concept of self-care is self-focused and doesn't include God, so it is secular rather than spiritual. Others believe that because God created our bodies in His divine image, and because Jesus, God the Son, took on human flesh, there is a spiritual link to how we live in our human body.

What is your opinion? Is self-care nothing more than a popular secular topic, or should Christian women take this as an important spiritual matter? Why?

In today's lesson, we will look at self-care as a spiritual practice because the Bible addresses the topic of our bodies and tells stories of how people used their bodies in ways that honored God as well as in sinful or harmful ways.

The spiritual practice of self-care recognizes that when you honor the body God created, you are honoring God.

Read 1 Corinthians 6:19. Who does your body belong to?

If God oversaw your body today, what would be the difference between how He would treat your body and how you treat your body? Fill in the columns below.

	How God would treat your body	How you treat your body
Sleep		
Exercise/ Movement		
Food		

In 1 Corinthians 6, Paul was writing to believers about the dangers of sexual sin. In verse 19, he makes the connection that how we use our bodies has an impact on our spirit, soul, and emotions. There are consequences to the choices that we make with our bodies.

As Christians, what are some negative things we do to our bodies but avoid talking about or holding each other accountable for?

The practice of self-care is anchored in the knowledge that we are caretakers of the bodies God created for us.

God has given you everything you need to win the battle of overwhelm in His power. But you must do your part by creating a practice that makes space for your God-given body to rest and be renewed. As Warren Wiersbe wrote, "If you begin each day by surrendering your body to Christ, it will make a great deal of difference in what you do with your body during the day."[5]

MEMORY VERSE MOMENT

Fill in the blanks for the memory verse as you continue to work on memorizing it.

Not that I was ever in need, ____ ___ ____ _____ ____ ___ ___

_____ _____ _____ ___ _____.

Philippians 4:11

PRAYER

God, today, I acknowledge that You are the creator and owner of my body. Please help me to love and care for my body as You love and care for me. In Jesus's name, amen.

CREATING A SPIRITUAL PRACTICE OF SELF-CARE

In today's lesson, we'll look at wisdom from Scripture that addresses how to care for our bodies, especially as we tend to neglect them when we're overwhelmed. Some of us grew up in environments where we were not taken care of by our parents, so we aren't sure that we deserve self-care. Others of us have dismissed self-care as a popular secular idea and have sacrificed ourselves in the name of loving God and others, but God never instructed us to do that. Let me add that for some, this spiritual practice may also require counseling, coaching, and accountability because you may have some contributing layers of past trauma or abuse that require personalized, gentle, restorative care.

I'll be using the acronym SELF as we discuss the four areas of self-care: sleep, exercise, laughter, and food. If you're also reading the *Stronger than Stress* book, you'll note that I cover a few different self-care topics as well. Feel free to pick one of these areas today and focus on implementing the biblical wisdom or practical tips as part of your lesson.

Sleep

When you're stressed, it's hard to sleep. However, we sometimes sabotage our sleep by staying up late scrolling on social media or trying to cram in housework. Our bodies are crying for more sleep! Lack of sleep also makes it harder for us to think. How many of us are trying to solve complicated problems with too little sleep? Also, insufficient sleep undermines good health. In one study, participants who slept less than six hours per night were 35 percent more likely to experience substantial weight gain. When we are sleep-deprived, our bodies release cortisol, the same stress hormone that pushes us into survival mode.[6]

Getting enough sleep enables us to come up with better solutions and make better decisions. In one study, a team of researchers asked participants to solve complicated math problems. The participants attempted to solve the problem and then were sent away for twelve hours. What the research revealed was that the people who slept well in that twelve hours were two and a half times more likely to solve the complicated problem when they came back to finish their work.

When you give your body permission to sleep, you are trusting God to take care of your world as you are in an unconscious sleep state.

Read Psalm 4:7–8. What is the writer trusting God to do?

What are some correlations or connections between trusting God and your current sleep patterns?

ACTION STEP: What are some sleep behaviors that you should be engaged in but have postponed?

Exercise

In his letters, Paul makes numerous references to sports, using athletic training as a metaphor for training in the Christian life (1 Cor. 9:24; Gal. 5:7; Phil. 3:13–14; 2 Tim. 4:8). In ancient times, athletes trained for the Olympic and Isthmian Games. These highly competitive events required lengthy training for optimal fitness. Self-discipline was a key factor in an athlete's training. This left an impression on Paul.

Read 1 Corinthians 9:27. What does Paul do for his body?

We don't know what kind of physical condition Paul was in. Remember his thorn in the flesh? If that was related to a bodily ailment, then physical activity may have been difficult for Paul. And yet Paul's body was his vehicle for ministry. To withstand his missionary journeys, enduring prison, physical abuse, and the rigors of ministry, Paul recognized that his body's fitness was part of living out his purpose.

We use our bodies to serve God and others. Some of you have hopes and dreams of being involved in certain ministries, starting businesses, or serving others in big ways. Is your body ready for such a task? As you pray about living out your purpose, preparing your body for the extra work, effort, and energy should be part of the planning.

As women, we endure so much social pressure to equate exercise with weight loss and physical appearance. We need to shift the conversation to include God's perspective on our bodies. Exercise is about moving our bodies so that we are physically prepared for God to move through us. Exercise isn't about how long you work out, how much you need to sweat, what you wear, or how much weight you lose. It's about moving your body in a way that's safe for you and that strengthens your bones and muscles. For me, walking is my go-to movement. I wear a fitness tracker watch that keeps track of my steps as I aim for my daily goal. I also use weights to strengthen my muscles. This helps me to withstand the rigors of traveling around the country in different time zones, the long hours of mental effort in writing, and the emotional load of the circumstances in my own life.

You need your body to do life. Furthermore, since we are integrated beings—mind, body, and soul—caring for our physical body can aid in our spiritual well-being. People who move their bodies only two days a week report a high degree of happiness and less stress, and numerous studies have reported that exercise is more effective than prescription medication at combating fatigue.[7]

ACTION STEP: What is a next step that you need to take with regard to exercise, whether you've been told by your healthcare professional or you sense an internal nudge or leading from God?

Laughter

When was the last time that you had a good laugh? When life gets to be too much, it's often because we stop making time for fun. During our family's long years of addiction crisis, every day was heavy with uncertainty and grief. As I watched circumstances out of my control steal from our family, my heart hurt each day. I knew that my kids were struggling too, so I began "Fun Saturdays." There was only one goal for Fun Saturday: we had to laugh.

Do you think that Jesus laughed? Yes. Did Paul laugh? I believe so. They had communities of people surrounding them, and I'm sure they weren't serious all the time, even if there were serious matters in their life.

Read Proverbs 17:22. How can a cheerful heart help you in hard times?

Do you need or do you already have the equivalent of Fun Saturdays? What does it look like for you to bring laughter and fun into your life?

ACTION STEP: What is a next step that you need to consider here?

Food

How we feed ourselves is an important part of how we care for our bodies. This is a complex issue, so this section will address a high-level scriptural principle. However, like the overall topic of self-care, you may need to enlist the help and support of counselors and coaches since stress-related and emotional-eating issues can have deep roots.

Read 1 Corinthians 10:31. What is Paul's teaching here?

This is where things get sensitive because comfort food is a socially acceptable way of coping with stress. When people are sick or lose a loved one, bringing over a dish or dropping off a freezer meal is a way of expressing love through food. However, there's a level of discernment that believers need to apply when it comes to our perspective on food.

Read 1 Corinthians 10:23. If you apply this to your dietary choices, what is Paul's point here?

As one who must be vigilant in her food choices, I understand and can relate to the magnetic draw of emotional eating. I spent years comforting my stress by indulging in special foods when I couldn't escape my problems, fears, anxieties, or overwhelm any other way. Even now, I still feel the pull toward all things creamy and sweet when I'm stressed, but Paul's teaching prompted me to establish some self-care boundaries, like only eating during certain hours, that reflect what I discern as the Holy Spirit's personal leading for me. Would you give the Holy Spirit the opportunity to lead you in this area?

ACTION STEP: What is a next step that you need to take with regard to food, whether you've been told by your healthcare professional or you sense an internal nudge or leading from God?

MEMORY VERSE MOMENT

It's the end of the week and time to write out the memory verse in the space below.

PRAYER

God, when it comes to self-care, there is so much to consider. Today, I'm praying for Your wisdom to know what You need me to prioritize. I am open to Your Spirit's guidance and conviction as well as making myself accountable in the areas where I need to practice self-care. In Jesus's name, amen.

Saying Yes to God

Submission • Sacrifice

MEMORY VERSE

Physical training is good, but training for godliness is much better, promising benefits in this life and in the life to come.

1 Timothy 4:8

RELYING ON GOD ALONE

We think you ought to know, dear brothers and sisters, about the trouble we went through in the province of Asia. We were crushed and overwhelmed beyond our ability to endure, and we thought we would never live through it. In fact, we expected to die. But as a result, we stopped relying on ourselves and learned to rely only on God, who raises the dead. And he did rescue us from mortal danger, and he will rescue us again. We have placed our confidence in him, and he will continue to rescue us. And you are helping us by praying for us. Then many people will give thanks because God has graciously answered so many prayers for our safety.

2 Corinthians 1:8–11

What are some of the emotions that Paul experienced during this time in his life?

What did Paul expect to happen to him and the others?

You might wonder what Paul faced that so overwhelmed him. While he doesn't mention a specific event, there are a number of trials that could apply here, including Paul's thorn in the flesh, having to deal with powerful men in Ephesus who were angry because Paul's preaching had affected their income (Acts 19:21–41; 1 Cor. 15:32), and physical persecution like the thirty-nine lashes that Paul received from the Jewish leaders (2 Cor. 11:24).[1] The bottom line is that Paul faced such stressful circumstances that he wasn't sure he'd survive.

Think of a time in life when you felt so crushed and overwhelmed that you weren't sure you could keep going. What was so hard about that season for you?

In the 1970s, Calgon launched their popular "Take Me Away" ad campaign that promised an escape for stressed-out people everywhere. I've had a few "God, please take me away" moments. I'm sure you have too. When we're overwhelmed, the desire to escape is real. During one overwhelming season, I often thought about what it would be like if a strong gust of wind swept me and my minivan off the bridge that I drove over twice a day. I didn't want to die, but I longed for an escape from that season of intense parenting, marriage struggles, stress at work, and exhaustion.

The term "passive suicidal ideation" describes the feeling of hating one's life but *not* planning to end it. It's a coping mechanism that can be triggered when one is under extreme stress. It speaks to the escapist desire for drastic change or for the stress in your life to go away. If at any point you experience passive suicidal ideation, it is important that you get extra support by speaking to a trusted friend, a counselor, or your healthcare provider.

NOTE: If you find yourself planning out specific methods to hurt yourself in a life-ending way, that is a giant signal that you need to call 988 for the National Suicide Prevention Hotline. The only thing you need to say is "HELP." Say that one word and God will bring people into your life to support you and help you see a path forward.

In Paul's case, the threat of death was very real, and he felt the emotional impact of that pressure. It's here we are reminded that just because we follow Jesus, it doesn't mean we won't experience seasons of too much. We all do.

Read 2 Corinthians 1:8–11 again. Circle the phrase "but as a result." What was the changing point for Paul and his companions?

Why is that important to Paul's decision to rely on God in stressful, dire circumstances?

Verse 10 is a pivotal point in which Paul tells his audience what changed for him and his companions. They shifted from overwhelmed and stressed to confident and peaceful when they stopped relying on themselves and started relying on God. He doesn't specifically say what they did, but I think that it's easy to relate.

In the left column below are some examples of relying on ourselves. Look up the verses about relying on God and fill in each blank with the encouragement or instruction on how to rely on God instead.

Relying on Yourself	Relying on God
Too busy to pray for God's help or wisdom.	James 1:5 _____
Trying to do too much in your own strength.	Psalm 28:7–8 _____
Attempting to control the outcome.	Matthew 6:34 _____
Ignoring God's instructions in Scripture or the leading of the Holy Spirit.	Luke 11:28 _____
Forgetting that God loves and cares about you, not just your situation.	1 Peter 5:7 _____
Facing spiritual battles without cooperating with God's power or protection.	2 Corinthians 10:5_____

Which of those verses resonated with you the most and why?

What is an overwhelming or stressful place in your life where you need to rely on God? What would that look like for you practically?

Paul ends this passage of Scripture by giving thanks for the people who are praying for him. He recognizes the gospel impact when his struggle causes people to pray and they can see God glorified through Paul's faith. The same goes for us. Our stress can be overwhelming, but when we ask others to pray for us, they follow our story. As we share about God's sustaining power and our reliance on Him, God uses our praise to plant a powerful testimony in the hearts of others.

In this week's study, you'll learn two new spiritual practices. These practices are essential and require you to open your heart, mind, and life to God at the deepest levels.

Is there a takeaway, a unique insight, or an aha moment from today's study that you'd like to remember?

MEMORY VERSE MOMENT

Write out this week's verse in the space below. Note any thoughts about this verse and how it can be applicable to your life today.

PRAYER

God, I need to rely on You today to face _____.
I will stop trying to handle it on my own and instead I will _____
_____ *so that You can step in. In Jesus's name, amen.*

LETTING GOD LEAD

SUBMISSION

So, I say, let the Holy Spirit guide your lives. Then you won't be doing what your sinful nature craves. The sinful nature wants to do evil, which is just the opposite of what the Spirit wants. And the Spirit gives us desires that are the opposite of what the sinful nature desires. These two forces are constantly fighting each other, so you are not free to carry out your good intentions.

Galatians 5:16–17

Circle the word "let." What does Paul mean when he says, "Let the Holy Spirit guide your lives"?

What does the Holy Spirit give us when we allow the Spirit to guide our lives?

One of the hallmarks of the Christian life is being led by the Spirit. In Galatians 5, as Paul teaches about letting the Holy Spirit guide our lives, the key word is "let." This implies that you have a choice as to whether or not you'll allow this. God gives us choices about how we live, but we also must bear the consequences of our choices. There are positive consequences that accompany obedience and negative consequences that follow with disobedience. In both instances, the consequences may not appear immediately, but Paul gives us insight into the fruit or outcomes that will happen in our lives at some point depending on how much or often we allow God's Spirit to guide our lives.

One criticism of Christianity is the false idea that a person needs to abandon their own agency in favor of being manipulated by others. But being led by the Spirit doesn't mean that you turn into a robot. Practicing submission is a choice and a freedom. It's a choice because God isn't making you do anything, and it's a freedom because the Spirit always leads us toward a rich and abundant life of faith and purpose.

Today's lesson delves into the spiritual practice of submission as reflected in Galatians 5. Submission is our willingness to be obedient to God. It's saying yes to God so that He can give us His best.

The incorrect teaching and practice of submission remains an embattled discipleship concept in the Christian life. Our human interpretation has warped God's definition into something that is not submission. Too many Christians have distorted submission into a self-serving demand to fit some human agenda. Submission has become a hammer when God designed it to be an invitation to holy blessing for His children.

However, just because some Christians have messed up submission doesn't mean that it is an irrelevant practice. We don't want to miss out on something good that God has for us just because of some bad actors. I know this spiritual practice will be challenging for some readers because you followed, trusted, and believed in spiritual leaders who did you wrong. In fact, the term "church hurt" refers to the emotional, spiritual, or abusive wounds that someone experiences within a Christian community. If this has ever happened to you, let me say that the hurt you've experienced or are now living through hurts the heart of God.

If I can say this gently, though: God wasn't the one who did you wrong. They did. God will hold them accountable.

Let's begin by reconstructing our understanding of the word itself. Submission is the joining of the prefix "sub" and the word "mission." "Sub" means to come under, not in the sense of having inferior value but of getting into a proper order.

The word "mission" is about having a purpose or goal. So then, submission is falling in line behind a purpose or goal. Submission is intended to be an act of free will, not force. Submission should also involve a worthy mission, not the whim of someone seeking to grab power or intimidate.

Read John 14:10 and John 14:31. How does Jesus submit to God?

Jesus understood the power of submission. Though equal with God, He willingly submitted to God's authority (Phil. 2:5–8). Godly submission doesn't diminish a person's self-worth or value. However, Jesus teaches us that we must deny our self-centered motives and demonstrate self-denial if we want to follow Him.

Read Mark 8:34. Why is submission necessary to be a follower of Christ?

Crucifixion was a crude method of execution that required the condemned to carry their own crossbeam to the place where they would be put to death.[2] Jesus created a graphic word picture of what it means for His followers to put to death personal agendas, self-determination, and pride. This act of denying ourselves happens when we first submit to Jesus as our Savior and Lord, but also at other times in our faith.

I can think of plenty of times when I've read something in the Bible that I felt I should do or sensed God leading me to do, but I didn't want to do it. Some examples include:

- forgiving those who hurt me
- holding my tongue when I really wanted to say something
- speaking up even when I felt nervous about it
- trusting God in tithing and finances
- showing up in places where God sent me even though I felt uncomfortable

From your own personal experience or from my list above, in what areas do you struggle or have you struggled to practice submission?

It's important not to lose sight of the blessing of practicing obedience. Yes, it can be hard to lay down what we want and let the Holy Spirit lead us. However, the joy of Spirit-led freedom is worth it! Whether you're releasing the pain of the past, asking forgiveness from sin, or finding a closer connection to God, there is a blessing waiting for you. Additionally, a Spirit-led life becomes a life filled with greater peace and purpose.

In tomorrow's lesson, you'll learn three words to help you start your submission practice.

MEMORY VERSE MOMENT

Fill in the blanks as you work on memorizing this week's memory verse.

_____ _____ is good, but _____ _____ _____ is much better, promising benefits in this life and in the life to come.

1 Timothy 4:8

PRAYER

God, Your way for my life is best. Help me to create a practice of submission so that I say yes to You before saying yes to myself. In Jesus's name, amen.

CREATING A SPIRITUAL PRACTICE OF SUBMISSION

Your own ears will hear him.
  Right behind you a voice will say,
"This is the way you should go,"
  whether to the right or to the left.
Isaiah 30:21

What does it look like practically to submit to God? It comes down to three words you'll learn today. Since the focus is on helping you with this practice, listen for the Holy Spirit's leading and notice if God is leading you in a particular decision or direction today.

In the Old Testament, there's a scene where the Israelites are preparing to cross the Jordan River into the promised land. God instructs Joshua and the leaders to take the ark of the covenant across first and then have the people follow.

Read Joshua 3:4. How far back were the people instructed to stay behind the ark?

The ark of the covenant was the physical symbol of the presence of God. I imagine that the Israelites were over the moon excited about entering the promised land after decades of wandering. However, I can also imagine they had questions about their new home. Perhaps some people had even started formulating plans about how to set up their new homes and what they would do for work.

God wanted to make it clear that He would guide them into the new land because "you have never traveled this way before" (Josh. 3:4). The same applies to us. How many times do we rush into something big and important after tossing up a quick prayer but without giving God adequate time to prepare us?

If we had to sum up God's instructions to the Israelites, it would be the three words that I mentioned you would learn at the start of today's lesson:

Let God lead.

Those three words capture the big idea of submission as the next spiritual practice. Submission is your willingness to be obedient to God and to let the Holy Spirit lead you. It's saying yes to God so that He can give His best to you.

Isaiah 30:21 at the beginning of today's lesson offers a prophetic glimpse into the future when God's people would be led by the internal guidance of the Holy Spirit rather than by the law.

Sometimes we mess up, so we need a tool to use when we fumble in our practice of submission.

Anytime our spiritual practice of submission wiggles off-track, we know it. It bothers us. It also creates a foothold for Satan to tell us lies about how disappointed God is in us and to make us question whether God still loves us.

What do you do when you blow it? How do you turn things around? The key is repentance. The Greek word for repentance is *metanoia*, which means a change of mind or a change in the inner person.[3] Repentance is saying, "God, I'm turning away from what I was doing and turning back to let You lead me."

Read Romans 2:4. How does God's prompting us toward repentance demonstrate His kindness and patience?

Repentance is a choice and a commitment that reconnects us with God.

While hurrying to an appointment one day, I was hustling down a side street in Savannah, Georgia, when I noticed a young man coming toward me with his head down. The streets weren't overly crowded, but there were a lot of people out walking. Yet, something about this young man caught my attention. I felt a nudge from the Holy Spirit whisper, "Tell him that God loves him."

My response was quick. "God, he's going to think that I'm weird."

I didn't want to be disobedient, but I also didn't want to look stupid.

As the young man passed by me in a crosswalk, my heart sank because I'd failed to do what I sensed God clearly asking me to do. A few moments later, I whirled around and projected my voice: "Excuse me."

The young man turned and looked at me.

I fumbled my words for a moment, which is unusual for me. I finally got myself together and spoke. "This might sound strange, but God wanted me to tell you that He loves you."

The young man's eyes widened and he tilted his head.

I shuffled my feet and looked down.

He spoke up. "Wow. That's wild. I'm having a really bad day. I needed to hear that today."

He didn't smile, but I could see that just a little heaviness around him had lifted. He turned and continued on his way.

Practical Steps: Creating a Practice of Letting God Lead

1. **Let God lead.** Train yourself to pray before big decisions and to leave plenty of space and time in advance for God to reveal or send discernment.

2. **Practice immediate obedience.** As soon as you sense God prompting you to say or do something, do it immediately. Delayed obedience is a temptation to disobedience.

3. **Practice self-denial in small ways.** When family or friends make reasonable requests for assistance, say yes to serving them and model submission.

4. **Don't delay repentance.** To keep the flow of connection with God, move toward repentance as soon as you are aware of your need to turn back toward God.

REFLECTION QUESTIONS

1. What are your takeaways from engaging in the practice of submission?

2. Is there a place in your life where you've postponed or outright declined a call to obedience?

3. As you reflect on yesterday's lesson and today's, is there a particular place of submission that stands out to you? What next steps do you need to take? Do you need to repent, pray for help, or step out in obedience?

MEMORY VERSE MOMENT

Fill in the blanks and keep working on memorizing!

Physical training is good, but training for godliness is much better,

_____ _____ in this life and in the

_____ _____ _____.

1 Timothy 4:8

PRAYER

God, reveal those places where I am slow to obey You and prompt my heart when repentance is necessary. In Jesus's name, amen.

GIVING UP FOR GOD'S HOLY GOOD

SACRIFICE

And so, dear brothers and sisters, I plead with you to give your bodies to God because of all he has done for you. Let them be a living and holy sacrifice—the kind he will find acceptable. This is truly the way to worship him.

Romans 12:1

When was the last time you gave up something that you love for something that you love more?

In our country, we're grateful for our armed services. The freedom that we enjoy today is because of the generations of soldiers who have sacrificed their lives for our freedom. As the mother of an Army officer, the knowledge that my child has made the decision to put their life on the line for our country terrifies me and fills me with pride all at the same time.

When you think about the word "sacrifice," what or who comes to mind?

What are some sacrifices that you've made in your life? What did it cost you? Why did you do it?

The spiritual practice of sacrifice is about giving up for God's holy good. Whatever God calls you to give up or lose is because He has plans to put His good in its place. His good doesn't always translate to a tangible blessing that you receive, and you may not even see the results in your lifetime, but He will do it. Maybe you are a grandmother who sacrifices an hour of sleep each morning to wake up and pray for your children and grandchildren, or maybe you are the person at church who has secretly funded a ministry for years. Those sacrifices don't go unnoticed by God.

Sacrifice is an extension of surrender. With sacrifice, you give up that which makes you feel secure or satisfied for something more valuable or important. Sometimes sacrifice is the first step in surrender, but that doesn't mean surrender is always a part of sacrifice. Sacrifice is also an outward expression of submission. You're letting God lead you toward giving up something so that you move toward living in His purpose for your life. There are also blessings, both tangible and intangible, that you will experience.

The Bible discusses sacrifice a lot. In the Old Testament, the first sacrifice occurred when God slaughtered an animal to make clothes for Adam and Eve after they sinned. When Moses received God's law at Mount Sinai, a formal sacrificial system was put into place for the people of Israel. Under that system, the people brought animals as offerings to God, and there were rules for what He considered an acceptable sacrifice. For example, God required the people to bring blemish-free animals and the best of what their fields produced. God knew their hearts and needed them to understand the seriousness of sin. For a sacrifice to be acceptable, it had to be something they valued highly. The irony is that whatever God called them to sacrifice came from His hand to begin with. "Sacrifice as worship is people giving back to God what God has previously given them as a means of grace."[4]

God implemented the Old Testament sacrificial system as a visual demonstration of the price of sin. In the New Testament, Jesus brought an end to animal sacrifices through His death on the cross.

Read Hebrews 10:10. What was the significance of Jesus's sacrifice?

Through His death and resurrection, Jesus brought an end to the need for a sacrificial system, even though the Jewish people continued to practice ritual animal sacrifice until the Second Temple was destroyed in AD 70.

As followers of Jesus, we make sacrifices to God in different ways. In Romans 12:1, Paul instructs us to offer our bodies as living sacrifices like Jesus did. Jesus gave up His life to redeem sinful people, and we're asked to give up our lives as well. Sacrifice doesn't always have to be a big thing, but it can be. However, there are lots of small ways to practice sacrifice throughout your day.

Additionally, you can offer a sacrifice by serving others. Depending on your life experience, you might already be doing this. In tomorrow's lesson, you'll learn some practical ways to practice sacrifice.

MEMORY VERSE MOMENT

Fill in the blanks as you work on memorizing this week's verse.

Physical training is good, but training for godliness is much better,

_____ _____ _____ _____ _____ _____ ____

_____ _____ ____ _____.

1 Timothy 4:8

PRAYER

God, thank You for the sacrifice that Jesus made on my behalf. I'm grateful that He gave up His life out of love for me. I want to offer You a continual sacrifice of praise in my life so that I can follow in Jesus's footsteps. In Jesus's name, amen.

CREATING A SPIRITUAL PRACTICE OF SACRIFICE

What is more pleasing to the LORD:
 your burnt offerings and sacrifices
 or your obedience to his voice?
Listen! Obedience is better than sacrifice,
 and submission is better than offering the fat of rams.

1 Samuel 15:22

God wants your heart more than He wants your sacrifice.

King Saul ignored this principle, but we can learn from his mistake. In 1 Samuel 15, God commanded King Saul and the Israelites to fight the Amalekites, who had rebelled against God for a long time. God instructed Saul to destroy everything.

The Israelites did fight the Amalekites and conquered them. However, Saul spared the life of Agag, the Amalekite king. Not only that, but the Israelites also saved the best of the Amalekites' animals—"everything, in fact, that appealed to them" (1 Sam. 15:9).

When the prophet Samuel confronted a cheery King Saul, the king replied that he was planning to sacrifice the animals to God.

Samuel's reply to Saul is recorded in 1 Samuel 15:22. Read that verse at the opening of today's lesson. Based on what you've learned from Saul's actions, why does God value obedience over sacrifice?

God cares more about your heart than about what you give up—or think you're giving up. King Saul and his men were greedy, and when they tried to cover up their sin as sacrifice, God saw right through it. Obedience is an act of submission that results in an act of sacrifice. It's possible for sacrifice to be a show we put on without being an act of praise.

Often, obedience is the sacrifice that God calls you to make.

As we explore the practical side of sacrifice, it might be helpful to revisit its definition: the spiritual practice of sacrifice is about giving up for God's holy good. Pay attention to the "why" of sacrifice: for God's holy good. We can make a lot of good sacrifices in life, but that doesn't mean they are for God. Also, we can make a lot of sacrifices, but that doesn't mean they are for our good either.

Some of you may feel like you're already making too many sacrifices. Maybe some of those sacrifices seem to be at the expense of your emotional, financial, and mental health.

Sacrifice is admirable, but it's not sacrifice if you're slowly destroying yourself. If you make too many sacrifices for too long and they aren't a clear directive from God, you run the risk of wrecking your health, your relationships, and your spiritual journey. God hasn't called you to sacrifice in a way that makes it difficult for you to live out kingdom priorities.

Is there a significant sacrifice that you've been making that you should continue, or do you need to pray about it, especially if it's causing overwhelm? Is it negatively impacting your health or creating conflict with others? List out some possibilities in the space below.

Read Hebrews 13:15–16. What do you think the writer means by "continual sacrifice of praise"?

What are two types of sacrifice that the writer mentions?

Our sacrifice of praise is every moment that we elevate God in our lives, whether it's through our obedience, our gratitude, or our service. Those are all sacrifices of praise. Why? As humans, we're inward focused. We're after what makes us feel good or helps us achieve our goals. Sacrifice is giving up for the sake of the gospel.

- We give up something to give ourselves over to God more fully.
- We give up something so that God can do more in others.

167

Sacrifice can also be material. In reflecting on Hebrews 13:15–16, Warren Wiersbe notes, "The word *spiritual* is not in contrast to *material*, because material gifts can be accepted as spiritual sacrifices."[5]

For me, the practice of sacrifice looks like my weekly fast. Food has a favorite place in my heart. However, emotional eating is an inside issue that tempts me to use food to comfort myself instead of turning to God. About a decade ago, God prompted me to fast one day a week. Each year, I prayerfully ask God if I should continue that sacrifice. As we saw in yesterday's lesson, God gave me the food that I am sacrificing back to Him. Fast day is hard for me. It has never gotten easier. However, in the place of my sacrifice, God has poured in a greater understanding of His love, a greater dependence on Him, and increased self-control. As God has filled the space of what I've given up, that prepares me to be used more for His good. Ultimately, I've gotten back exponentially more than God has asked me to give up.

Here is an opportunity for you to plan out an interactive way to practice sacrifice. In the list of ideas below, put a check mark beside the one you'd like to practice either today or in the coming week.

Practical Ideas for Sacrifice

- Fast once a week and use those mealtimes to pray, study the Bible, or listen to worship music.
- For one or two days a week, spend your lunch hour praying or listening to worship music instead of scrolling social media or running errands.
- Reduce your standard of living so you can increase your giving and devote more time to serving.
- Be open to hosting an exchange student with your family and pray for an opportunity to share the gospel with them.
- Give up a week of work and serve on a missions trip.
- Give up your lunch once a week and donate the money to a gospel-centered organization, then use the time you would have been eating to pray for them.
- Take one day per month and serve. (If you're already doing one day, increase that!)

- Offer to babysit for a single parent.
- Invite each person in your family to sell an item of value and as a family choose where to donate the money.

Do you have any other ideas? List them below:

- _____

- _____

- _____

- _____

REFLECTION QUESTIONS

1. How could the practice of sacrifice draw you closer to God?

2. What hesitations or struggles do you have when considering this practice?

3. Are there any adjustments you could make so that this practice would be more meaningful and sustainable for you?

MEMORY VERSE MOMENT

Write out this week's memory verse in the space below.

PRAYER

God, thank You for modeling sacrifice by giving up Jesus for my earthly and eternal good. As I'm reflecting on what You may be asking me to sacrifice, I pray for the conviction and courage to follow wherever You are leading me. In Jesus's name, amen.

Overcoming Together!

Sisterhood • Celebration

MEMORY VERSE

Two people are better off than one, for they can help each other succeed.

Ecclesiastes 4:9

FROM STRESSED TO BLESSED AFTER THE STORM

When you go through deep waters,
  I will be with you.
When you go through rivers of difficulty,
  you will not drown.
When you walk through the fire of oppression,
  you will not be burned up;
  the flames will not consume you.

Isaiah 43:2

It's our final week together. In this final week, we'll look at Paul's ship-wreck and time on Malta before learning about the final two spiritual practices: sisterhood and celebration. I'm sharing this story about Paul because it's a final reminder of his tremendous faith in times of intense stress.

In Acts 23, God tells Paul that he will go to Rome to preach the gospel. However, Paul's journey to Rome took a roundabout path as he first spent a few years in prison, was shipwrecked, and then had to spend a winter on the island of Malta.

We won't have time to study all the fascinating layers of this story, but it reads like an action-adventure novel, so read the entire story on your own in Acts 27–28. You'll note that Paul's adventure wraps up the book of Acts.

While Paul was imprisoned, he shared the gospel with two Roman governors, Felix and Festus (Acts 24–25), and he also had a chance to speak with King Agrippa when he came to town. Paul again relayed the gospel message and his testimony. Agrippa is almost persuaded to believe the gospel, but not quite. In a contentious moment, Paul demanded his rights as a Roman citizen to appeal his case to Caesar. Festus granted his request (Acts 25:11), but the writer of Acts records a postscript in which Agrippa says, "He could have been set free if he hadn't appealed to Caesar" (Acts 26:32).

So Paul boarded a ship headed to Rome.

Read Acts 27:1–12. According to verse 9, what made this voyage so challenging?

In verse 10, what does Paul tell the ship's officers?

When Paul predicted what was going to happen, who did the officer in charge of prisoners listen to instead of Paul?

Paul was grouped in with the prisoners on the boat. However, as New Testament scholar N. T. Wright notes, there was something quite peculiar at the start of Paul's journey to Rome: "The really strange thing about Paul's voyage to Rome is the way in which Paul himself appears to take charge."[1] I laughed when I read that, because Wright makes it sound like Paul was bossy. Even though Paul was considered a prisoner, he had not been convicted of a crime. The Roman officers would have been puzzled by this man who was accused of matters that didn't make sense to them and how eager he was to plead his case in Rome. Not only that, but Paul had an entourage traveling with him.

Rome was a bustling city and needed lots of food and goods. It's likely that the ship's officers didn't listen to Paul because they were carrying enough grain to justify the risk of a voyage so late in the year. If there weren't many other boats bringing in grain or other food, the ship's captain and owner stood to make a lot of money on that transport.

One commentator observed that Paul's assertion about the likelihood of a bad outcome wasn't so much a prophetic insight as an informed warning based on the fact that he had been shipwrecked twice already (2 Cor. 11:25–26). He'd seen conditions like this before.[2]

Read Acts 27:13–26 and answer the following questions:

Why did the sailors tie ropes around the boat's hull? What else did they do to slow down the ship? (v. 17)

What did the crew begin throwing overboard the next day? What did they toss overboard the day after that? (vv. 18–19)

Imagine the conditions in verses 20–21. If you were on the ship, what would you be stressed about?

Can't you just see the ship's owner and captain cringing as they watched the crew toss the precious grain overboard? I imagine their minds would have bounced back and forth between wondering if they'd ever see their families again and the likelihood of financial disaster if they did survive.

In verse 37, we're told that there were 276 people on board the ship. Imagine the sense of unanchored-ness everyone must have felt to be in complete darkness on the water. Imagine their irritability from fear and hunger. Imagine the stench of anxious sweat and their anger from the lack of control.

Paul decides to call a team meeting. Again, Paul was just some curious man on the boat that the crew didn't know. Yet, they recognized him as a man of influence, so they listened to them.

What does Paul tell the crew in verse 22? Notice the word "courage."

While Paul begins with a little "I told you so" in verse 21, he launches into a message of hope in the darkness on the stormy seas. Even though the ship will go down, Paul lets everyone know that they will all survive.

Read Acts 27:33–37 and answer the following questions:

What was the condition of the people on board? (v. 33)

What did Paul tell them to do? How did they feel afterward? (vv. 34–36)

Let me just say that I'm impressed how Luke records the number of people on the ship. That was a lot of stressed people wondering if they were going to survive and worrying about their families. Yet, the simple act of eating some food along with Paul's words of encouragement made a difference.

A few verses later, the ship begins to break apart after running aground too soon. The soldiers want to execute all the prisoners to prevent them from escaping, but the commanding officer won't allow it (Acts 27:41–44). We don't want to gloss over the fact that Paul would have lost his life if the soldiers had their way. God had to intervene. "According to the Code of Justinian, a Roman guard who allowed a prisoner to escape could face the same penalty awaiting the accused prisoner."[3] Why did the commanding officer want to save Paul's life? There's no way to know for sure. However, I wonder if he believed Paul's prophecy that everyone would be saved and if he perhaps admired Paul or even felt curiosity about Paul's gospel message.

Just as Paul had assured them, everyone makes it safely to shore on the island of Malta. The adventure continues as Paul miraculously survives a snakebite. Publius, the island's chief official, welcomes everyone and shows them hospitality, and Paul heals Publius's sick father as well as many other sick people on the island. After losing everything in the shipwreck, there was a good ending to Paul's time on the island.

Read Acts 28:10. How did the people on the island respond to Paul and his entourage when it was time to leave for Rome?

In times of stress, God can surround us with people from unexpected places to help us. Sometimes, we're so focused on what's going wrong that we may miss or reject the people God has sent to answer our prayers.

When you've been in difficult circumstances, who are some of the people who have been a blessing to you?

How has that made a difference to you?

MEMORY VERSE MOMENT

Write out this week's memory verse in the space below.

PRAYER

God, thank You for the people that You've sent me at various times when the storms of life seemed to tear everything apart. If life is stormy now, remind me that You are always present and help me see where You're taking care of me. In Jesus's name, amen.

BETTER TOGETHER

SISTERHOOD

Two people are better off than one, for they can help each
other succeed.

Ecclesiastes 4:9

What does Ecclesiastes 4:9 teach you about the value of having others
in your life?

Depending on your background, that verse might feel like it's rubbing salt into your friendship wounds. Most of us can recount stories of friends who didn't have our back, but that doesn't mean that God's teachings about community aren't true and good for you. Today, I'm going to ask that, whether you are carrying old or even fresh friendship wounds, you will give God a chance to speak a fresh, maybe even healing message into your heart.

The spiritual practice of sisterhood is committing to use your connection to Christ to create strong bonds with other sisters in Christ. Yes, the body of Christ is made of men and women who love Jesus, but sisterhood fulfills a specific need in the life of an overwhelmed woman. With one or two or a group of other women, a stressed or overwhelmed woman knows that there are sisters who have her back and who will remind her that God does too. After all, who knows better than other women how a woman is feeling?

While in prison, Paul often wrote about the people who came and cared for him. Those friends and visitors lifted his spirits. At the end of 2 Timothy, Paul lists a number of specific individuals in his circle of connection. These people were committed to Christ, and that commitment fueled their connection to Paul.

In the opening of his letter to the Romans, Paul gives us insight into how he operates in Christian community with other believers:

> For I long to visit you so I can bring you some spiritual gift that will help you grow strong in the Lord. When we get together, I want to encourage you in your faith, but I also want to be encouraged by yours. (1:11–12)

In these two verses, Paul mentions four ways that he wants to share community:

1. He desires to _____ them.

2. He wants to bring a spiritual gift to help them grow

   _____.

3. He wants to _____ them.

4. He is willing to be _____ by them.

One takeaway that stands out for me is that Paul couldn't do much for his friends while he was in prison. When Paul wasn't in prison, there were times when his commitment to the gospel landed him and his friends in some tricky situations. Even though Paul couldn't host his friends for dinner, buy them gifts, or come over to help them out with projects or pick up the kids, he invested in their spiritual needs, which would make a difference in other areas of their lives.

Yet, Paul knew that Christian community would never be perfect. We are human and therefore we can say or do things that hurt each other.

I'm tagging in another leader in the church, Peter, to remind us of what can bind us together when our imperfections threaten to tear our relationships apart. In his time with Jesus as one of the twelve disciples, Peter experienced the beauty and bumps that can occur in Christian community. Yet, he also had the advantage of Jesus as the perfect model for how to live in community with others.

Read 1 Peter 4:8–10. When it comes to community with other imperfect believers, why do we need love? What is it about love that covers a multitude of sins?

How does showing up and using your gifts help those in your community (v. 10)?

Community is not about keeping score, which is something that can often ruin friendships. In friendship, there can be a conscious or unconscious quid pro quo attitude of "you do something for me and I'll do something for you." Peter's teaching puts the focus on you and not worrying about what others are doing. This means that there will be times when it looks imbalanced and you're giving more than you're receiving. And there will be other times when you'll receive more.

During the long, difficult years after my separation and the healing period after my marriage ended, my sisterhood circle gave me far more than what I could give them. Friends supported me via countless prayers, visits, texts, flowers, and hugs. One friend met me at McDonald's for an hour every other week, and I would cry most of that time. Inside, I hated that my friends were giving so much when I had so little to give back, but they gave out of the abundance that Christ had given them.

Read Matthew 4:11. What did Jesus allow the angels to do?

This is one of my favorite aha moments in Scripture. It blew me away to realize that even Jesus allowed others to come and minister to Him. He didn't have to, but He did. Sisterhood recognizes that we'll all face ups and downs, but we can be there for each other—even when we do it imperfectly. Can we clothe ourselves with forgiveness, grace, and good boundaries and try again?

Did you have any aha moments today? Note any new insights or leadings from God in the space below.

Has there been something holding you back from fully engaging in sisterhood as a practice? Is there a conversation you need to have, an offense you need to surrender, or a courageous step you need to take to reach out?

MEMORY VERSE MOMENT

Fill in the blanks for the final memory verse of the study:

_____ _____ are better off than one, for they can _____ _____ other succeed.

Ecclesiastes 4:9

PRAYER

God, thank You for creating us to connect with each other. It's not easy, especially when there have been hurts and disagreements. Open my heart to how I can be obedient to Your desire for me to be a part of a healthy sisterhood and reflect the gospel in our sisterhood community. In Jesus's name, amen.

CREATING A SPIRITUAL PRACTICE OF SISTERHOOD

SISTER CARE

So encourage each other and build each other up, just as you are already doing.

1 Thessalonians 5:11

For those of us who love our Christian sisters, this spiritual practice seems like a no-brainer. Maybe all of your friends are from your church and you've been together longer than the last three pastors at your church combined. It might be tough for you to imagine that there are Christian women out there whose worst nightmare is showing up for a women's small group. But it's true.

For those who enjoy sisterhood, a big high five to you! If God has given you a beautiful sisterhood, pray about how He might use you to help more women find what you have.

For those who struggle with sisterhood, today's study is for you.

Which group do you belong in?

Once you've been burned, it's tough to reengage. I've been there on multiple occasions. I remember being so close to leaving my church because I felt completely invisible and unloved. For a few weeks, I acted like a porcupine with quills to keep people from hurting me. I'd come and go from church without talking to anyone. If anyone did greet me, my replies were only one or two words. I'd glare at the people who hurt me and have all sorts of imaginary conversations in my head.

In our effort to protect ourselves from future pain, we sometimes hurt ourselves more by avoiding connection. To be clear, the hurt is real, but healing can only happen in safe Christian community with other believers surrounding us. In my case, God provided a women's leadership mentoring group that I joined.

Jesus's half brother James offers divine insight into how God uses other believers to help us when the brokenness of our world breaks us.

Read James 5:16. What two instructions does James teach to those in community?

What is the outcome of praying for each other?

Think of the troubles that you hear about in the world regarding loneliness, isolation, and mental health. Much of that can be traced back to people not having a safe place to be open, validated, supported, and pointed back to Jesus. Sure, people can hop on social media and talk about their deep problems and pain, but where is the healing? Where is the life transformation? Others may offer support in the comments, but that's not enough for what a person really needs to heal.

Read Colossians 3:12–14 below and circle the qualities that identify us as God's people.

> Since God chose you to be the holy people he loves, you must clothe yourselves with tenderhearted mercy, kindness, humility, gentleness, and patience. Make allowance for each other's faults, and forgive anyone who offends you. Remember, the Lord forgave you, so you must forgive others. Above all, clothe yourselves with love, which binds us all together in perfect harmony.

Read the second and third sentences again. What does Paul imply about the imperfections of community?

Paul has given us the framework for what healthy, safe Christian community looks like. We can be together . . . and toxic. Paul's goal is for us to be better *together*.

People will make mistakes and things can get messy. We all mess up at times, but it is Jesus who holds us together. In Paul's teaching, he expects people to live in the flow of the Holy Spirit, not our human efforts. Why? Our human efforts are not adequate. Community can be hard, challenging, lopsided, and disappointing. We need supernatural mercy, kindness, humility, gentleness, and patience, as well as supernatural forgiveness and love.

If we're going to practice sisterhood as a godly spiritual practice, it's essential that we understand what makes for a safe sisterhood, otherwise we'll pop up our quills and go it alone. Here are five principles for creating safety so you can practice sisterhood with others and experience the power and blessing of community:

1. **Keep coming back.** Make a commitment to each other to show up on a regular basis and to not cancel when life gets difficult or inconvenient. If a problem comes up, Jesus gives instructions in Matthew 18 on how to work through problems safely and effectively with other believers.

2. **More listening and learning, less lecturing.** There's nothing wrong with sharing Bible verses, especially since it's the Word of God. However, it's important to listen first and really hear what a sister is saying before you launch into what you want to say—especially when she is overwhelmed or stressed. You don't have to fix her, just listen.

    It's helpful to ask her questions like, "What's hard about this for you?" and "What are you praying about these days?" Such questions send her the message that she's cared for, and they give you greater insight into her situation. With insight, you can know how to pray for her, and if the door opens for you to speak, you can do so with wisdom.

3. **Pray for each other and check on each other.** This should come as no surprise, but I'm mentioning it anyway. Prayer is your most powerful act of love. The latter part of James 5:16 teaches that the prayer of a righteous person is powerful and effective. So, if you have a sister who is under a great deal of stress, your prayers are a needed source of support for her. If you've ever been prayed for by someone, you've likely exhaled from the relief of being lifted up in prayer. We want to make sure that we prioritize that gift.

4. **Keep confidence.** Complete confidentiality is the key to safe sisterhood community. It's helpful to remind each other on a regular basis, "What we say here, stays here."

5. **Bring your best and think the best of others.** You aren't in control of how others behave in community, but you are in control of how you behave, and you are accountable to God. Bring your best. Live out what Scripture teaches about community by

inviting the Holy Spirit to work through you. Think the best of others and their motives. Trust that the Holy Spirit is working in them even if you can't see it.

REFLECTION QUESTIONS

1. As you think about the spiritual practice of sisterhood, what has been your experience?

2. What would healthy Christian sisterhood look like for you?

3. How can you engage with this practice this week? Ideas include inviting a trusted Christian friend to have coffee, sending a text message to encourage a woman in your Bible study group or at work, or praying for one friend a day. Write down what you will do in the space below.

MEMORY VERSE MOMENT

Two people are better off than one, _____ _____ _____

_____ _____ _____ _____.

Ecclesiastes 4:9

PRAYER

God, please help me to see, experience, and model sisterhood and community. Show me where I need to bring a healthier attitude toward community, extend forgiveness, or take that first step in opening myself up to meet others. In Jesus's name, amen.

GOD LOVES A PARTY!

CELEBRATION

> Be thankful in all circumstances, for this is God's will for you who belong to Christ Jesus.
>
> 1 Thessalonians 5:18

I once discovered a significant mistake in a writing project. It was the kind of mistake that would require hours to fix—hours that I hadn't planned on. So I decided to head to the library where I could leverage a change of scenery as I jumped in.

My community's downtown library is an award-winning space with high ceilings, lots of plants, and the quiet-busy hum of pages turning and librarians padding from one area to another. As I walked from the parking garage to the main level, I mentally prepared myself to dig in. But my thoughts were interrupted by the sound of a bass guitar and drums. As I stepped off the elevator, I heard amplified voices. I walked toward the sound and discovered there was a lunchtime concert in the main atrium that day.

The band played one popular cover after another. As good as they were, however, the best part for me was watching the audience: dozens of summer camp kids, multiple pockets of intellectually challenged individuals from various group homes, and the regular crowd of unhoused individuals who spend their days in the library.

There in the atrium, we tapped our feet, danced, or swayed in our seats to the music (not everyone on rhythm). The best way I can describe it is to say that we were celebrating life together.

The joy of that experience refilled my energy. As the band ended their set and people started to leave, I couldn't stop smiling.

There's nothing like a good party. But an even better party is when God's people are gathered in His name.

I don't know if you know this, but God is the original party planner. He thought of everything for His people, including making celebrations and festivals. One of the earliest examples in the Bible is after God freed the Israelites from centuries of slavery. God not only delivered them from physical and mental bondage but also instituted a new tradition of celebration. His people again had the opportunity to freely worship Him, but God's brand of celebration also gave them the chance to do the things we all love to do when we celebrate—eat, connect, enjoy music, and even dance.

Read Leviticus 23:1–2. What did God appoint for His people?

In Leviticus 23 we read God's instructions for seven festivals that He commanded all Israelites to participate in. Celebration wasn't limited to those who met certain requirements. God wanted everyone to experience it. The festivals provided an opportunity for the people to remember God's great deeds in delivering them from Egypt and leading them through the wilderness.

In many ways, celebration can strengthen our faith. When we take time to reflect on and rejoice in what God has done, it uplifts our heart and fortifies us for the next stretch on the journey. Perhaps celebration is needed more than ever during stressful seasons!

Read 1 Thessalonians 5:18 at the beginning of today's lesson. Why does God want you to give thanks in good times and bad times?

In Luke 15:11–32, Jesus tells a story about a young man who leaves his family, disgracing his parents and wasting his inheritance. After recognizing that his father's servants were living better than him, the young man decides to return home, hoping that he could work as a servant. As the son approaches, the father sees him in the distance and runs to his son. After the son confesses his sin toward his father, Jesus delivers the plot twist of a surprising celebration that would have shocked His audience.

Read Luke 15:22–24. What does the father command his servants to do? In verse 23, what does he say they will all do?

The father calls for a celebration because his son has returned. This would have shocked Jesus's audience because they would not have deemed the son worth celebrating. After all, the son had brought shame to the family. But the father doesn't care. He celebrates his son, not his son's actions.

Jesus told this story to illustrate God's great heart for those who are far from Him, but it also speaks to those of us who believe that we must work for our reward or for celebration.

How do you feel about being celebrated, whether it's your birthday or another party given in your honor?

If you've had a hard time being the center of attention, can you identify or list some reasons why?

In tomorrow's lesson, you'll learn four principles to help you experience the joy of practicing celebration. The more you do it, the more you should enjoy it and the more you can see God's blessing in your life!

What have you learned today about how God sees celebration that has been an aha moment or inspired you?

MEMORY VERSE MOMENT

Two people are better off than one, for _____ _____ _____
_____ other succeed.

Ecclesiastes 4:9

PRAYER

*God, give me a heart for celebration! I don't want to just throw a
party, but I want You to be the center of my rejoicing. Thank You for
Your generosity in my life. I want to celebrate that as often as I can.
In Jesus's name, amen.*

CREATING A SPIRITUAL PRACTICE OF CELEBRATION

On your feet now—applaud GOD!
  Bring a gift of laughter,
    sing yourselves into his presence.

Psalm 100:1–2 MSG

When my kids were growing up, it was hard getting everyone home in the evenings to celebrate birthdays. After a few years of frustration, I decided that we'd celebrate birthdays at breakfast since we were all home in the morning. I'd wait until everyone went to bed and then decorate the kitchen or dining room with streamers, hang signs, and run to the store to pick up cake and ice cream. The next morning, we'd circle around the person we were celebrating and sing "Happy Birthday" before eating cake and ice cream at 7:00 a.m. We kept up this tradition through the rest of their school years, and what had started as a frustration became a unique family tradition. Who doesn't love morning cake?

Over the years, I've been intentional to model celebration for my adult kids. I'm proud that they live out the value of celebration in their lives.

This final lesson is a poignant subject to wrap up our time together as you learn practical tips and ideas for practicing celebration in your own life. It's been an honor to travel this season with you. Talking about celebration is a wonderful way to end our time together!

Celebration is a form of gratitude that we practice when we recognize the evidence of God's goodness and create an intentional moment around it. The goal of this lesson is for you to recognize how you can practice celebration as a regular part of your life.

Let's look at four principles for the spiritual practice of celebration.

1. Incorporate gratitude as a celebration of your daily life.

> But I will give repeated thanks to the Lord,
>   praising him to everyone. (Ps. 109:30)

Gratitude is the fuel for celebration. In a message that I shared on gratitude years ago, I taught the audience a lesson that God taught to me: *Giving God thanks in everyday things trains you to give God thanks for all things.* When you stop and acknowledge God's presence, power, and provision each day, that strengthens your heart against discouragement when tough seasons come.

In my early days as a mom, there was a long season when money was tight. I remember when our family came out of that season and funds flowed freely again. I began a habit back then that I continue today. Whenever I pay for my groceries, I have a silent celebration right in the checkout line before I pay. I pray, "God, thank You for the provision that made it possible to purchase this food. Thank You for the work and for the money that I've earned." It's simple, but it's a celebration that happened because of God.

2. Invite God to be a part of your rejoicing because He's the one who made it possible.

> Yes, the Lord has done amazing things for us!
>   What joy! (Ps. 126:3)

You have because God gives to you. In every celebration, whether it's a holiday, a family birthday, or the end of the workweek, God should be an honored guest. You can honor God by acknowledging Him in prayer, by having everyone write on a card something that God has done, or by sharing stories of God's faithfulness.

3. Prepare yourself and rest up so that you can enjoy it.

It's hard to celebrate when you're tired. If you are planning a celebration, there's a temptation to burn the candle at both ends to make everything perfect. However, perfection isn't the goal of celebration. Your engaged presence is far more important.

Read Leviticus 23:7. What does God instruct the people to do on the first day of the festival?

God knew that His people had worked hard, and He wanted them to rest up before starting the festival celebrations. If you practice Sabbath, you'll have that opportunity to rest, but if you still need to begin that practice, I hope that looking forward to incorporating celebration into your life is a motivator.

4. Don't skimp on celebration.

When Jesus attended the wedding in Cana and the host ran out of wine, Jesus's mother prevailed upon Him to help. Jesus turned water into wine, but the exclamation point on this miracle is that the wine He created was a most delicious, impressive vintage. A surprised master of ceremonies tasted Jesus's wine and proclaimed the following:

> "A host always serves the best wine first," he said. "Then, when everyone has had a lot to drink, he brings out the less expensive wine. But you have kept the best until now!" (John 2:10)

Christians have differing opinions about alcohol, so this observation has nothing to do with your personal convictions. I'm simply making the point that Jesus didn't skimp at a celebration.

When engaging in this spiritual practice for yourself, invest in the celebration. I'm not saying that you should empty your monthly budget, but as women we tend to put ourselves last.

Whenever I turn in a manuscript to a publisher, I like to celebrate by going for a walk at the park, getting ice cream, taking myself out to lunch, or—my favorite—booking a massage. Of all those options, the massage is the most expensive. There are times when I've made myself book the massage. It was an expensive treat that I could afford, but the real point was that I needed to celebrate what God had done on a level that was meaningful and memorable to me. When you skimp or cheap out on celebration, then you might not take it seriously because it didn't require much investment.

MEMORY VERSE MOMENT

Write out this week's memory verse in the space below.

FINAL PRAYER

Today's prayer is a little different. Shortly after I began writing books, I started to include a blessing at the end of each book or Bible study. It wasn't planned. On one project, it was around midnight and the Bible study was due first thing in the morning, and I didn't know how to finish it. I prayed and asked God for help because I didn't know what to do. There was a whisper in that moment reminding me that when I meet with women in Bible study, the last thing that we do is pray. So that's where the tradition of this final benediction was born.

May God's grace and peace go before you,
May His strength and mercy meet you,
And may you never, ever forget . . .
God is with you.
God is for you.

God will never fail you.
God sees beyond what you can see.
God can carry what you can't.
God IS the way when you can't see your way.
God promises His presence.
God will provide for you.
God will anchor you.
God will always love you.
In Jesus's name, amen.

NOTES

Introduction

1. American Psychological Association, "Stress in America 2022: Concerned for the Future, Beset by Inflation," press release, October 2022, https://www.apa.org/news/press/releases/stress/2022/concerned-future-inflation.

Week One Too Many Spinning Plates

1. Moyer Hubbard, "2 Corinthians," *Zondervan Illustrated Bible Backgrounds Commentary*, ed. Clinton E. Arnold, vol. 3, *Romans to Philemon* (Grand Rapids: Zondervan, 2002), 253.

2. F. F. Bruce, *Paul: Apostle of the Heart Set Free* (Grand Rapids: Eerdmans, 1977), 34–35.

3. Bruce, *Apostle of the Heart Set Free*, 37.

4. *Strong's Concordance*, s.v. "7965. *shalom*," Bible Hub, accessed May 19, 2023, https://biblehub.com/hebrew/7965.htm.

5. *Strong's Concordance*, s.v. "1515. *eiréné*," Bible Hub, accessed May 19, 2023, https://biblehub.com/greek/1515.htm.

6. David Guzik, "2 Corinthians 12—The Strength of Grace in Weakness," Blue Letter Bible, accessed July 26, 2023, https://www.blueletterbible.org/comm/guzik_david/study-guide/2-corinthians/2-corinthians-12.cfm?a=1090007.

7. Guzik, "2 Corinthians 12."

8. Warren Wiersbe, *The Wiersbe Bible Commentary: New Testament* (Colorado Springs: David C Cook, 2007), 539.

Week Two Getting Out of Survival Mode

1. Barb Roose, *Surrender: Letting Go and Living Like Jesus* (Nashville: Abingdon, 2020).

2. Richard J. Foster, *Celebration of Discipline*, 25th anniversary ed. (New York: HarperCollins, 1998), 30–31.

3. S. P. Carter, K. Greenberg, and M. S. Walker, "Should Professors Ban Laptops? How Classroom Computer Use Affects Student Learning," *Education Next* 17, no. 4: 68–74.

Week Three De-Stressing Your Thoughts

1. Jason Murdock, "Humans Have More Than 6,000 Thoughts per Day, Psychologists Discover," *Newsweek*, July 15, 2020, https://www.newsweek.com/humans-6000-thoughts-every-day-1517963.

2. Quoted in Michael Bergeisen, "The Neuroscience of Happiness," *Greater Good Magazine*, September 22, 2010, https://greatergood.berkeley.edu/article/item/the_neuroscience_of_happiness.

3. Elisabeth Elliot, *Keep a Quiet Heart* (Grand Rapids: Revell, 2022), 215.

4. Adam Macinnis, "Report: 26 Million Americans Stop Reading Their Bible Regularly During COVID-19," *Christianity Today*, April 20, 2022, https://www.christianitytoday.com/news/2022/april/state-of-bible-reading-decline-report-26-million.html.

5. Wiersbe, *Wiersbe Bible Commentary: New Testament*, 812.

6. *Strong's Concordance*, "2656. *chephets*," Bible Hub, accessed June 12, 2023, https://biblehub.com/hebrew/2656.htm.

Week Four Bringing God's Peace to Stressful Places

1. "Home Organization Is Major Source of Stress for Americans, Survey Finds," *HuffPost*, May 22, 2013, https://www.huffpost.com/entry/home-organization-stress-survey_n_3308575.

2. Microsoft, "Introducing Microsoft To-Do," accessed July 19, 2023, https://www.youtube.com/watch?v=6k3_T84z5Ds.

3. Foster, *Celebration of Discipline*, 85.

4. Wiersbe, *Wiersbe Bible Commentary: New Testament*, 24.

5. Wiersbe, *Wiersbe Bible Commentary: New Testament*, 471.

6. Tom Rath and James Harter, *Well-Being: The Five Essential Elements* (New York: Gallup Press, 2014), 83.

7. Rath and Harter, *Well-Being*, 78–79.

Week Five Saying Yes to God

1. David Guzik, "2 Corinthians 1—The God of All Comfort," Enduring Word, accessed May 25, 2023, https://enduringword.com/bible-commentary/2-corinthians-1.

2. "Cross," *Nelson's Illustrated Bible Dictionary: New and Enhanced Edition*, ed. Ronald F. Youngblood (Nashville: Thomas Nelson, 2014), 282.

3. *Strong's Concordance*, s.v. "3341. *metanoia*," Bible Hub, accessed November 9, 2023, https://biblehub.com/greek/3341.htm.

4. "Sacrifice," *Nelson's Illustrated Bible Dictionary*, 1005.

5. Wiersbe, *Wiersbe Bible Commentary: New Testament*, 844.

Week Six Overcoming Together!

1. N. T. Wright, *Paul: A Biography* (San Francisco: HarperOne, 2018), 374.

2. Clinton E. Arnold, "Acts," *Zondervan Illustrated Bible Backgrounds Commentary*, ed. Clinton E. Arnold, vol. 2, *John, Acts* (Grand Rapids: Zondervan, 2002), 472.

3. Arnold, "Acts," 477.

BARB ROOSE is an author, a speaker at national women's conferences, and a regular contributor to (in)courage, Crosswalk, and iBelieve. She has written five Bible studies and four books and writes a weekly Happy Monday devotional. Barb serves as a teaching pastor at her home church with over 6,000 in weekly attendance. The proud mother of three adult kids, Barb loves reading and walking. Whenever possible, she prefers to eat dessert first.

Connect with Barb:

BarbRoose.com

 @barbararoose

 @barbroose

COMBAT CHRONIC STRESS, BURNOUT, AND OVERWHELM BY DEVELOPING
10 SPIRITUAL PRACTICES

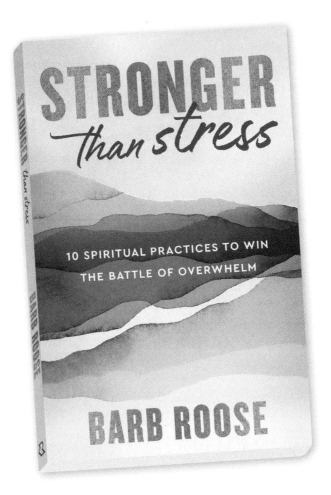

- **Learn** the four main stress triggers
- **Discover** exercises to help you interrupt your fight-or-flight stress response
- **Study** the apostle Paul's life and teachings as he models how to deal with daily overwhelm
- **Win** the battle of overwhelm by utilizing spiritual practices
- **Wake up** each day with confidence that you can live at peace and in wholeness

Revell
a division of Baker Publishing Group
RevellBooks.com

Available wherever books and ebooks are sold.